Praise for Spork-Fed and the Spork Sisters

"Jenny and Heather have truly spiced up vegan cuisine, making it modern, appealing, and approachable for anyone looking to eat healthy food without sacrificing flavor. I always look forward to my trips back to L.A. to enjoy a meal with them."
CHEF TAL RONNEN, *NYT* BEST-SELLING AUTHOR, *THE CONSCIOUS COOK*

"Spork Foods has taken vegan food to a whole new level! Their recipes are creative, delicious and very doable at home!"
ED BEGLEY JR., ACTIVIST AND STAR OF "LIVING WITH ED" ON PLANET GREEN

"I found Spork Foods to be tasty, fresh and delightfully carcass-free. Two stars! (out of two, so hey ... pretty good!)"
AL YANKOVIC (WEIRD AL), SINGER-SONGWRITER, ACTOR, COMEDIAN

"Their positive energy is infectious! They make you excited about all of the yummy, healthy and cruelty-free options out there."
ALEXANDRA PAUL, FILM AND TV ACTRESS, ACTIVIST

"The best thing each of us can do to make a difference for animals, as well as ourselves and the planet, is to adopt a vegan lifestyle. Heather and Jenny's upbeat approach shows you how enjoyable and easy vegan cooking is. Compassion never tasted this good!"
GENE BAUR, PRESIDENT AND CO-FOUNDER, FARM SANCTUARY

"Heather and Jenny are an exciting addition to the vegan scene ... they make veganism look goooood!"
SARAH KRAMER, AWARD-WINNING COOKBOOK AUTHOR, INCLUDING *HOW IT ALL VEGAN*
CREATOR OF GOVEGAN.NET

Spork-Fed

Spork-Fed

SUPER FUN AND FLAVORFUL VEGAN RECIPES
FROM THE SISTERS OF SPORK FOODS

Jenny **ENGEL** & Heather **GOLDBERG**

st. lynn's
press
PITTSBURGH

Spork-Fed

Super Fun and Flavorful Vegan Recipes from the Sisters of Spork Foods

ISBN: 978-0-9832726-1-8

Library of Congress Control Number: 2011928752
CIP information available upon request

First Edition, 2011

St. Lynn's Press . POB 18680 . Pittsburgh, PA 15236
412.466.0790 . www.stlynnspress.com

Book design and typesetting – Pure Design, www.getpuredesign.com
Editor – Catherine Dees
Editorial Intern – Karen Masnica

Photo and Art Credits

Cover photograph: ©Jiro Schneider, www.jirophoto.com
Food photography: ©Patrick M. Gookin II, www.patrickmgookin.com
Photography art direction, illustrations and damask pattern: Kevin Tseng, www.kevintseng.com
Dedication page photograph: ©Lauren Virdone, www.laurenvirdone.com

Disclaimer

The authors and publisher expressly disclaim any responsibility for any adverse effects occurring as a result of the suggestions or information herein, including the handling or consuming of ingredients and foods named in this book. For all medical questions the reader should consult the appropriate health practitioners.

Printed in the United States of America on triple-certified FSC, SFI, and PEFC and 10% PCW Sterling Ultra Gloss paper.

This title and all St. Lynn's Press books may be purchased for educational, business, or sales promotional use. For information please write:
Special Markets Department . St. Lynn's Press . POB 18680 . Pittsburgh, PA 15236

10 9 8 7 6 5 4 3 2 1

Dedication

This book is dedicated to our inspirational family,
whom we love more than anything in the whole world.

Table of Contents

Foreword

We grew up watching our mother bake bread almost every day. She took great care (and still does) assembling all the ingredients, kneading the dough, and watching it rise. Because we witnessed this passion and joy for preparing food all through our lives, it's easy for us to recognize the same spirit in others. That is why we love Heather and Jenny. They embody this spirit when they are cooking. They light up a whole room with their enthusiasm, and inspire everyone around them to get excited about cooking as well. It's absolutely infectious.

Vegans, vegetarians and omnivores alike will fall in love with these fabulous sisters and their amazing food. It's about time they share their passion for food with the world!

EMILY: I first found out about the Spork sisters a few years back when a close friend recommended Spork Foods cooking classes. Back then, Jenny and Heather were teaching in Silver Lake, California, with themes as broad as rolling your own sushi, creating French crêpes, and veganizing Passover. I loved walking into the cozy atmosphere with these girls, who seemed more like vegan fairies than human beings, laughing their way through the class. I walked away with a belly full of tasty food and a brain full of nutritional knowledge to take home with me. As a long-term vegan, I have read about nutrition for years, but these girls exposed me to so much I had never heard about!

ZOOEY: Emily has been vegan since high school, and though I'm not vegan (I tried but didn't succeed), I do have multiple food allergies. Both Emily and I are committed to maintaining a healthy lifestyle without giving up flavor. That's why we love the Spork sisters! They're passionate about delicious food that just so happens to be good for you.

EMILY: Also, just look at their cute faces on the cover! How could you not love those adorable girls?!

ZOOEY: Like me, there are plenty of non-vegans in the Spork cooking classes who come looking to add more vegetables and whole grains into their diets without feeling deprived.

EMILY: After I had attended a few classes I had the sisters cater my birthday party. I am drooling now, thinking about the mac and cheese they made (recipe inside!), and the pink lemonade cupcakes!

ZOOEY: However you have found yourself holding this book in your hands, you're in for a real treat; one you can feel good about.

We encourage everyone to pick up this book and take the Spork adventure!

The Deschanel Sisters

Emily and Zooey Deschanel

Introduction

Everyone's path in life is different. Some people know from a very young age that they want to grow up to be a doctor, actor, teacher, or dancer. When we were young, we knew we wanted to run our own sister business— although the focus of our biz didn't take shape until we both became vegan.

At college our eyes were opened to the global impact and political context of our food choices, and we felt strongly enough to start making a statement with every meal. Heather (older sis) transitioned to veganism first, and Jenny, who had been vegetarian since high school, soon followed.

Jenny later trained at the Natural Gourmet Institute in New York City and Heather helped run an 11,000-member environmental nonprofit organization, which gave us the formal training and real-world experience we needed to kick-start our vegan sister biz.

We love cooking and everything it embodies. When you make a meal, it's the perfect excuse to bring together friends and family. And when you make vegan dishes that appeal to all types of people, even better. That's why we started our company, Spork Foods, where we provide cooking classes, private lessons, and healthy-eating consultations. We pride ourselves on creating recipes that are approachable, easy, and irresistible to all sorts of palates—cooking that blows the minds of not only vegans, but vegetarians, omnivores and die-hard meat eaters too. Even though a lot of people might have preconceived notions of vegan food, all it takes is one tasty meal to change their opinions forever. We call it "delicious persuasion"—you can't fight it!

Food is more than proteins mixed with carbs and fats, and it's more than just a meal. Food is powerful. It's a huge part of all our traditions, celebrations, religions, health, energy and self-image. By getting to know an array of people through our cooking classes, we've discovered that many of us feel guilty about eating "bad" foods. So when we cook, we make recipes that are satisfying, sometimes decadent, and always animal-ingredient- and cruelty-free —because that's how we choose to live our lives.

Our students keep us going and constantly motivate us to develop exciting new recipes. Some of our favorite moments are when a student tells us how much healthier or more energized he or she is feeling, thanks to our recipes—or how successful our meals are with his or her entire non-vegan family. When students share their culinary successes or ask us questions about what we know and love, it truly makes our job the best job in the world. We're thankful for being able to teach people how to cook, and it means so much to us to be living our sister business dream.

As soon as students started flying in from Seattle, Texas, and even Japan to take our classes in Los Angeles, we decided it was time to also put ourselves on the web. We launched Sporkonline.com to give the world a fun and engaging website where people can experience vegan cooking and a vegan lifestyle on their own time.

Every food has a history, and many of the natural ingredients mentioned in this book have medicinal qualities that have been coveted for thousands of years. In the "For Your Smarts" and "For Your Parts" sections that accompany each recipe, you'll learn a little more about how different cultures appreciate these foods, and what these ingredients do for your health. You'll never look at an eggplant the same way again! (Not to spoil the surprise, but technically—it's a berry! Wow!)

Use this book to have fun in the kitchen. Our recipes are designed to build your confidence and let you enjoy cooking and, of course, eating. We cover recipes from all over the globe because we want to show how expansive the flavors are in the vegan world. Many of the recipes here are gluten-free, too. You can have it all! And if you've been searching far and wide for a vegan version of your favorite dish to no avail—well, hopefully this cookbook will give you the boost you need to "veganize" it on your own, making a meal that's healthier and friendlier to animals and the planet than the non-vegan equivalent.

We strive to present a cuisine that is modern and sophisticated, as we want anyone who picks up this book to feel proud to serve these dishes to anyone lucky enough to sit at your table.

Thank you for taking the time to enjoy *Spork-Fed!*

Sincerely,

Jenny and Heather

P.S. When you see a number at the end of a "For Your Smarts" or "For Your Parts" section, make sure you turn to the Notes section in the back of the book for extra info.

P.P.S. Check out our suggested menus on the following pages for a little creative meal planning!

Suggested Menus!

Here are some sample menus that we love — to kick-start your meal planning and inspire you to get cooking!

Happens to be Gluten-Free

Velvety Carrot Soup with Mint Oil p. 30 + **Patatas Bravas** p. 50 + **Creamy Pistachio Pesto over Brown Rice** p. 110 + **Crème Fraîche and Berry Parfait** p. 154

Throwback to the '50s

Creamy Tomato Soup p. 42 + **Green Bean Casserole with Spelt Bread Crumbs and Frizzled Shallots** p. 55 + **Frosted Tempeh Loaf** p. 104 + **Apple Pie Milkshake** p. 130

Fancy Pants

French Onion Soup with a Cheesy Crouton Topping p. 32 + **Cashew Cream Fettuccine Alfredo with Sautéed Spinach and Cheese Crisps** p. 96 + **Ginger, Maple and Mustard-Glazed Tempeh** p. 124 + **Apple and Pear Tarte Tatin** p. 128

Brunch O'Clock

Tempeh Bacon-Stuffed Potato Pom Poms p. 178

Chive and Cheddar Skillet Omelet p. 168

Strawberry Cream Cheese-Stuffed French Toast p. 165

Toasted Pecan Spelt Coffee Cake p. 176

Hold Me—Comfort Foods

"Fried" Green Tomatoes p. 68

Creamy Baked Macaroni and Cheese with a Spelt Bread Crumb Topping p. 122

South Carolina Barbecue Tofu Sandwich p. 114

Strawberry Shortcakes with a Coconut Whipped Cream Topping p. 144

Get Stuffed—Thanksgiving

Broccolini in a Pecan Brown "Butter" Brandy Sauce p. 74

Green Apple and Cashew Sourdough Stuffing p. 70

Seitan Wellington with a Creamy Spinach Sauce p. 88

Pumpkin Cheesecake with a Gingersnap Crust p. 156

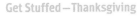

Suggested Menus!

Happy Holidays!

Creamed Onions with a Whole Wheat Bread Crumb Topping p. 52

Mashed Potatoes with Caramelized Onions and Crispy Sage p. 66

Personal Seitan Pot Pies with an Herb Biscuit Topping p. 98

Chocolate Mint Truffles p. 158

Fresh, Fast & Healthy

Quinoa Salad with Fennel and White Beans in a Light Lemon Vinaigrette p. 60

Chilled Creamy Red and Yellow Gazpacho p. 36

Cornmeal and Herb-Crusted Tofu Feta Croquettes p. 112

Grandma's Bird's Nest Cookies Rolled in Pistachios p. 132

Good for the Whole Fam

Green Salad with Creamy Tempeh Bacon Ranch Dressing p. 34

Southwest Black Bean and Corn Mini Burgers p. 79

Grilled Asparagus with an Herb Pine Nut Sauce p. 64

Chocolate Peanut Butter Mousse with a Crunchy Topping p. 134

Asian Foods Gone Vegan

 **+**  **+**  **+**

Tofu Satay with a Decadent Peanut Sauce p. 4

Vietnamese Crêpe with a Mushroom-Bean Sprout Filling p. 94

Crispy Brown Rice Cakes with Adzuki Beans and Scallions p. 58

Crispy Green Tea Cookies p. 138

As Decadent as It Gets

 **+**  **+**  **+**

Beer-Battered Tempeh Fish with a Tartar Sauce p. 22

Spicy Seitan Buffalo Wings p. 6

Twice-Baked Potatoes with a Broccoli and Cheese Filling p. 72

Crunchy Peanut Butter Bonbons p. 140

It's My Party and I'll Cook If I Want To

 **+**  **+**  **+**

Amazing Caesar Salad with Homemade Croutons p. 28

Pear, Fig and Sage Tarts with a Roasted Garlic Aioli p. 2

Barbecue-Style Spelt Pizza with Caramelized Onions and Tempeh Bacon p. 116

Vanilla Birthday Cake with a Buttercream Frosting and Sprinkles p. 150

Talkin' Sporkie

Food doesn't always have to mean serious business! When we're teaching cooking classes, we have fun in our kitch, with our students, and when we don't feel like being technical—we use our Sporkie terminology. Here's a glossary of some of our fave Sporkie-isms, so you can start speaking our language!

Appie	Appetizer	**OMG**	Oh My Gosh
Avo	Avocado	**Peepers**	Eyes
B-day	Birthday	**Peeps**	People
Bod	Body	**Redic**	Ridiculous
Broc	Broccoli	**Rep**	Reputation
Cals	Calories	**Snoresville**	Something boring, or uninteresting
Crampies	Menstrual cramps	**Surezies**	Sure
Druff	Dandruff	**Toots**	Flatulence
Fam	Family	**V-day**	Valentine's Day
Fave	Favorite	**Vacay**	Vacation
Grody to the Max	Something that's very gross or disgusting	**Veganize(d)**	When you substitute vegan ingredients for non-vegan ones
Hubby	Husband	**Viteys**	Vitamins
Kitch	Kitchen	**Wifey**	Wife, spouse
Mins	Minutes		

APPETIZERS

*(gf) indicates the recipe is gluten-free!

Pear, Fig and Sage Tarts with a Roasted Garlic Aioli

This little flavor threesome is really something to talk about. Take the tarts to a party as an appetizer or make them larger and serve this dish as an entrée. If you've been looking for one perfect, crunchy bite to encompass all of the flavors of fall, look no further! **Yields 10-12 tarts**

Roasted Garlic Aioli Ingredients

6 cloves garlic
(see roasting directions)
Dash neutral tasting high-heat oil
1 cup vegan mayonnaise
2 teaspoons fresh lemon juice
1 teaspoon agave nectar
¼ teaspoon sea salt, plus dash
¼ teaspoon finely ground
black pepper, plus dash

Tart Ingredients

2 D'Anjou pears, cut to ½-inch pieces
10-12 leaves fresh sage,
finely chopped
5-6 dry Black Mission figs, sliced
2 teaspoons fresh lemon juice
1-2 sheets frozen puff pastry, thawed

Directions

For the roasted garlic: Preheat oven to 350°F. Slice off base of bulb with a large chef's knife (just less than half an inch). Place bulb, cut side down, in an oiled heat-proof baking dish and sprinkle with sea salt and black pepper. Roast for about 25-30 minutes, or until cloves are soft. Set aside.

Turn oven up to 425°F.

For the aioli: Remove roasted garlic cloves from pan. Place on cutting board and smooth with flat side of a chef's knife, creating a paste. Transfer to a large bowl and add mayonnaise, lemon juice, agave, sea salt and black pepper. Whisk until uniform. Set aside.

For the filling: Place sliced pears, sage and figs in 3 separate bowls. Coat pear slices in lemon juice to prevent browning, and set aside.

Cut thawed puff pastry into 2- or 3-inch squares.

On each square, place about 1 teaspoon garlic aioli, a pinch of sage and 1 piece each of fig and pear, reserving about 2 tablespoons aioli for serving. Bring up corners to center of square. Carefully squeeze to seal puff pastry. Repeat for all squares.

Line a baking sheet with parchment paper or a silicone baking mat (or use cooking spray).

Place each tart on the baking sheet, about ½ inch apart and bake for about 18-20 minutes, or until tarts are lightly browned.

To serve, top each tart with about ½ teaspoon aioli. Garnish with fresh chopped sage for presentation.

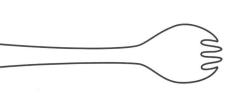

The Sporkie Scoop

FOR YOUR SMARTS The flavor and texture of pears actually improve after they are picked — just the opposite of most fruits!

FOR YOUR PARTS Figs have incredible blood sugar-stabilizing properties and can lessen some diabetics' need for insulin.[1]

Tofu Satay with a Decadent Peanut Sauce (gf)

Drizzle peanut sauce on anything and it tastes good, right? Making your own peanut sauce is quick and simple, and these skewers make a wonderful side dish or appie. Use the sauce to sexy up some brown rice and veggies if you have some left over, or just eat it with a spoon when no one is looking. **Yields about 12 skewers**

Tofu Ingredients

1 (14-ounce) block extra-firm tofu (see homemade tofu recipe on p. 84)

2 tablespoons rice vinegar

1 tablespoon neutral tasting high-heat oil, plus 2 tablespoons

1 tablespoon palm sugar or evaporated cane sugar

2 tablespoons tamari (wheat-free)

¼ teaspoon garlic powder

½ teaspoon finely ground black pepper

Peanut Sauce Ingredients

¾ cup peanut butter

½ cup regular coconut milk

1 cup water, more or less, as needed

¼ cup tamari (wheat-free)

3 tablespoons maple syrup

¼ cup rice vinegar

2 tablespoons sesame oil (with or without chilies)

2 tablespoons fresh lime juice, plus grated zest of 1 lime

2 tablespoons pickled ginger, finely chopped

3 cloves garlic, finely chopped

2 tablespoons red pepper flakes (optional)

Directions

Press tofu gently with a clean towel to remove excess moisture. Slice block of tofu horizontally into two rectangles. Slice each rectangle in half and cut diagonally, creating smaller triangles. Place tofu triangles in a baking dish. Add vinegar, 1 tablespoon oil, sugar, tamari, garlic powder and black pepper to the tofu triangles, and coat them evenly. Marinate tofu for 10-30 minutes, turning over occasionally.

Heat a grill pan or large sauté pan and add remaining oil. Cook over medium-high heat for about 3 minutes on each side, or until grill marks appear, if using grill pan. Place one or two tofu triangles on each skewer and set aside.

For the peanut sauce: In a small (2-quart) pot, combine peanut butter, coconut milk and about ½ cup warm water. Whisk until peanut butter is smooth and uniform. Add tamari, maple syrup, vinegar, sesame oil, lime juice and zest, pickled ginger, garlic and red pepper flakes, if using. Stir until smooth. The sauce should be fairly dark. Heat sauce through for about 5-7 minutes over low heat, adding more water if sauce appears too thick, and set aside.

Pour sauce into a bowl and place on a large platter with the tofu skewers.

The Sporkie Scoop

FOR YOUR SMARTS Satay is commonly thought to have originated in Indonesia. If you want to make it more authentic, use the inner piece of a coconut palm frond as your skewer.

FOR YOUR PARTS Palm sugar is a great substitute for refined, granulated sugar because it is a pure sweetener made from the dried nectar of the coconut palm tree. It is packed with vitamins and is considered a low glycemic sweetener. We use it not only because it is natural and unrefined, but because it's really rich and delicious!

Spicy Seitan Buffalo Wings

Sometimes people think that vegan food isn't "man food," but this dish is spicy and crunchy, and you can eat it with your hands — so it's definitely man-approved. These make a super fun party snack — and if you're cooking for a crowd that can take the heat, toss in some habañero peppers or scotch bonnets and make 'em breathe fire! **Serves 6-8**

Seitan Ingredients

½ cup whole wheat pastry flour

½ cup unbleached all-purpose flour

½ teaspoon cayenne pepper

½ teaspoon sea salt

½ teaspoon finely ground black pepper

½ teaspoon garlic powder

1 teaspoon evaporated cane sugar

3 cups "chicken-style" seitan, or homemade seitan (see recipe on p. 86)

2 tablespoons neutral tasting high-heat oil

Buffalo Wing Sauce Ingredients

2 heaping tablespoons non-dairy butter

1 large red bell pepper, diced

2 ripe red jalapeño peppers, diced

½ brown onion, finely chopped

3 cloves garlic, finely chopped

1 teaspoon paprika

1 teaspoon sea salt

½ teaspoon celery seed

½ teaspoon parsley flakes

Dash freshly grated nutmeg

¼ cup soymilk creamer

¼ cup unfiltered apple cider vinegar

½ cup water

Directions

Preheat oven to 400°F.

In a large bowl, combine flours, cayenne, sea salt, black pepper, garlic powder and sugar, and whisk. Add seitan pieces and coat in flour mixture. Reserve 1 tablespoon flour mixture for sauce.

Place coated seitan pieces on a baking sheet and drizzle with oil. Bake for about 25 minutes, or until coating is crisp, turning them over once, halfway through baking.

For the sauce: While seitan is baking, in a large (6-quart) pot add butter, peppers, onion, garlic, paprika, sea salt, celery seed, parsley flakes and nutmeg. Add reserved 1 tablespoon coating flour mixture. Cook on high heat for about 3 minutes, stirring occasionally.

(continued on next page)

Spicy Seitan Buffalo Wings

(continued from previous page)

Directions (continued)

Add soymilk creamer, vinegar and water and cook about 5 minutes, or until peppers are soft. Transfer to a blender and blend sauce until smooth. Remove center of your blender lid to allow heat to escape. Cover blender opening with a cloth towel. Set sauce aside.

To serve, coat warm seitan in sauce. Serve warm.

Note: If you do not have a blender, use a food processor to make this sauce.

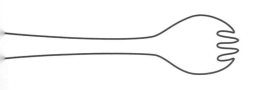

The Sporkie Scoop

FOR YOUR SMARTS Capsaicin is the component in chilies that makes them spicy and hot hot HOT. In 1912, a pharmacist named Wilbur Scoville came up with a way of measuring the units of heat in chilies: the Scoville scale. So what is the hottest pepper on the scale? The Naga Viper, measuring a whopping 1,359,000 units! That's about 500 times hotter than a jalapeño!

FOR YOUR PARTS Celery seeds aren't just delish, they are also an amazing diuretic and can help treat health issues like gout. They assist your body with eliminating uric acid buildup.[2]

Chickpea Cakes with a Sweet Truffle Drizzle (gf)

These gluten-free cakes are our spin on the traditional socca cake, or farinata, that originated in Genoa, Italy, and are served in certain parts of France. Sometimes they are made in a large, round pan and baked in the oven at about 500°F, but we find that making them as small, individual sized pancakes on the stovetop does the trick! And when you add the truffle drizzle? Mamma mia! **Yields about 16 cakes**

Chickpea Cake Ingredients

2 tablespoons egg replacer, dry

2 cups chickpea (garbanzo bean) flour

½ teaspoon non-aluminum baking powder

1 teaspoon sea salt

¼ teaspoon finely ground black pepper

¼ teaspoon turmeric

½ teaspoon herbes de Provence

1½ cups vegetable broth (low-sodium)

1 tablespoon neutral tasting high-heat oil, plus ⅓ cup for cooking

2 teaspoons fresh lemon juice

Sweet Truffle Drizzle Ingredients

2 teaspoons fresh lemon juice, plus grated zest of 1 lemon

1 teaspoon truffle oil

1 tablespoon agave nectar

2 tablespoons brown rice syrup

½ teaspoon sea salt

¼ teaspoon finely ground black pepper

Fresh thyme for garnish

Directions

In a large bowl, whisk egg replacer, chickpea flour, baking powder, sea salt, black pepper, turmeric and herbes de Provence until uniform. Add vegetable broth, 1 tablespoon oil and lemon juice. Heat a large sauté pan and add ⅓ cup oil. Carefully spoon 1 tablespoon of mixture at a time into oiled pan and cook over medium heat until slightly browned, about 2-3 minutes, or until bubbles appear. Flip and cook for an additional minute or until golden.

Set aside on a greased cookie sheet if not using right away.

For the truffle drizzle: Whisk together lemon juice and zest, truffle oil, agave, brown rice syrup, sea salt and black pepper until uniform, and set aside.

To serve, plate chickpea cakes as desired and pour a small amount of truffle drizzle over each cake. Top with finely chopped fresh thyme for presentation.

Note: To reheat chickpea cakes, place them in a 350°F oven for about 5-7 minutes.

The Sporkie Scoop

FOR YOUR SMARTS Truffles are a fungus that grows 3-12 inches underground near the roots of trees! Truffle oil usually has an olive oil base with truffle essence. With hundreds of varieties, black and white truffles are highly prized, but there are other kinds that intrigue us, like pecan truffles, which grow in pecan orchards!

FOR YOUR PARTS Chickpeas have a lesser-known trace mineral in them with a cute long name, molybdenum. Our bods need this to detoxify sulfites, which are a preservative and not good for us! Other foods have molybdenum too, such as lentils, peanuts and peas.[3]

Corn Cakes with a Smoky Paprika Sauce (gf)

These light and crispy corn cakes are perfect either as an appie or side dish for any meal. The paprika sauce is really incredible on top, and you can also use it as a dip for veggies, or even as a salad dressing. **Yields 8-10 cakes**

Corn Cake Ingredients

1 tablespoon egg replacer, dry

1 cup chickpea (garbanzo bean) flour

½ teaspoon non-aluminum baking powder

½ teaspoon sea salt

¼ teaspoon finely ground black pepper

¼ teaspoon turmeric

½ teaspoon dried thyme

½ teaspoon barbecue spice

⅔ cup unsweetened almond or soymilk

2 teaspoons neutral tasting high-heat oil, plus 1 tablespoon for pan

2 teaspoons fresh lemon juice

2 teaspoons agave nectar

1 cup corn kernels (frozen, or kernels from 2 ears fresh corn)

Smoky Paprika Sauce Ingredients

⅔ cup vegan mayonnaise

1-2 tablespoons unsweetened almond or soymilk

2 teaspoons brown rice syrup

1 tablespoon fresh lemon juice

½ teaspoon smoky paprika

¼ teaspoon sea salt

¼ teaspoon finely ground black pepper

Directions

In a large bowl, whisk egg replacer, chickpea flour, baking powder, sea salt, black pepper, turmeric, thyme, barbecue spice, almond or soymilk, 2 teaspoons oil, lemon juice and agave. Add corn kernels and stir to coat.

Heat a large sauté pan and add remaining oil. Carefully spoon 1 tablespoon at a time of corn cake mixture into oiled pan, keeping a slight separation between cakes. Cook over medium heat until slightly browned, for about 2 minutes or until bubbles appear in top of each cake. Flip and cook corn cakes for an additional minute.

If not using cakes right away, set aside on a greased cookie sheet and reheat in a 375°F oven for about 7-10 minutes.

For the sauce: Combine mayonnaise, almond or soymilk, brown rice syrup, lemon juice, paprika, sea salt and black pepper in a bowl and whisk. To allow flavors to develop, refrigerate for about 30 minutes before serving.

The Sporkie Scoop

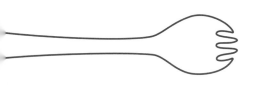

FOR YOUR SMARTS Paprika is made by grinding dried chili pepper pods, and when the peppers are smoked for days, you get the rich taste of smoky paprika. Hungarian paprika is very popular because it is considered the finest available.

FOR YOUR PARTS Corn contains lutein, a carotenoid (meaning "natural color or pigment") that promotes skin and eye health![4]

Coconut and Lime Seitan Skewers

This appetizer is so summery and refreshing — and easy! The flavor combination of coconut and lime is always a good idea, especially in the form of a crunchy seitan appie. Make these for any potluck or picnic and people will be surprised at how much flavor you can pack onto one little skewer! **Serves 4-6**

Ingredients

1 (14-ounce) can regular coconut milk

2 tablespoons fresh lime juice, and grated zest of 1 lime

1½ teaspoons jerk seasoning or spice rub

¼ teaspoon sea salt

2 tablespoons brown rice syrup

2 packages seitan stir-fry strips, or 3 cups homemade seitan pieces (see recipe on p. 86)

1 tablespoon neutral tasting high-heat oil

½ cup finely shredded coconut

Directions

Mix coconut milk, lime juice and zest, jerk seasoning, sea salt and brown rice syrup in a large bowl and whisk until uniform. Cut seitan into 1- or 2-inch pieces and marinate pieces in mixture for 30 minutes to overnight.

Preheat a large sauté pan and add oil. Pour seitan and mixture into pan. Cook over medium heat for about 5-7 minutes on each side, until well browned.

The liquid will not evaporate until seitan is well cooked, so use it to keep glazing seitan in pan. Cook for about 5 additional minutes, until all liquid has been absorbed.

To serve, place shredded coconut in a shallow dish. Place 2-3 pieces of seitan on each skewer, and roll in shredded coconut. Serve warm.

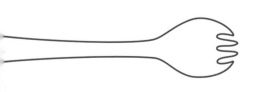

The Sporkie Scoop

FOR YOUR SMARTS One popular type of lime used in cooking is the Key lime, which gets its name because of its cultivation in the Florida Keys. The limes were originally brought to the Americas and parts of the Caribbean by European explorers in the 1600s.

FOR YOUR PARTS About a third of the world's population depends on coconut to some degree for their food and economy. Coconut oil is thought to aid in preventing osteoporosis because it helps your bod absorb and retain calcium and magnesium![5]

Lentil Pecan Pâté (gf)

This pâté is a wonderful appetizer when served with crackers or crudités. You can also use it as a filling for sandwiches or wraps. We often teach this recipe in our "get your protein" class because the lentils and pecans are super high in protein, giving you a great energy boost! Many peeps have told us that this is a better version of, and closely resembles, chopped liver. Our dad loves this pâté and refers to it as our "mock choppy." But in all honesty, we've never tasted the non-vegan version — nor have we come within about 10 feet of it. Pee-eww! **Serves 8-10**

Ingredients

4 cups water

¾ cup dried green lentils

Dash sea salt, plus 1½ teaspoons

1 bay leaf

2 tablespoons neutral tasting high-heat oil, plus 1 tablespoon

1 large yellow onion, finely chopped

6-8 crimini mushrooms, diced

Dash finely ground black pepper, plus ½ teaspoon

½ cup toasted pecan pieces

¼ cup fresh lemon juice, or vegan white wine

4 sprigs fresh thyme, or 5-6 leaves fresh sage, finely chopped,

3 carrots and/or celery ribs, cut into sticks for crudités

1 package organic non-hydrogenated crackers (optional)

Directions

In a medium (4-quart) pot, add water, lentils, sea salt and bay leaf. Cover and bring to a boil over high heat. Turn heat to low and simmer, uncovered, for 20-25 minutes or until lentils are tender.

Meanwhile, in a large (6-quart) pot, add 2 tablespoons oil and sauté onion and mushrooms over medium heat until slightly browned. Sprinkle with a dash of sea salt and black pepper.

Add mushroom mixture and toasted pecans to a food processor, and set aside.

When lentils are cooked, drain and remove bay leaf. Add lentils to food processor with mushroom and pecan mixture. Add remaining sea salt, black pepper, lemon juice or white wine and either thyme or sage.

Pulse together for about 30 seconds, or until well mixed. Using the feed tube, drizzle in additional oil. Pulse until smooth.

Transfer to a large bowl. Pâté will keep in refrigerator for up to 3 days.

When serving, spoon into a small bowl and place on a platter surrounded by crudités or optional crackers. Garnish with fresh herbs.

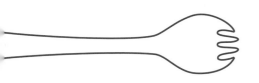

The Sporkie Scoop

FOR YOUR SMARTS Crimini mushrooms are baby portobellos! All types of mushrooms have been eaten for thousands of years. Ancient Egyptians thought that mushrooms made you immortal, and only the pharaohs were allowed to eat them!

FOR YOUR PARTS Lentils may be a legume, but they don't have sulfur in them, so they won't make you into a gas machine like other beans can!

Nachos with a Melty Cashew Cheese, Lemon Herb Sour Cream and Guacamole (gf)

These nachos are fun to make for a party and can feed a crowd in no time flat. And this cashew cheese is redic! It's melty and gooey, and can firm up in the refrigerator IF you have leftovers (the chances of this are slim to none). For dramatic effect, pour the cheese on the chips while your guests are watching, and listen to them "ooh" and "aah." **Serves 6-8**

Cashew Cheese Ingredients

3 cups unsweetened almond or soymilk

¼ cup agar agar flakes

1½ cups cashews

1 teaspoon garlic powder

¾ teaspoon sea salt

¼ teaspoon smoky paprika

1 tablespoon light miso paste (non-barley)

¼ cup nutritional yeast flakes

2 teaspoons agave nectar

2 teaspoons neutral tasting oil

2 teaspoons fresh lemon juice

Lemon Herb Sour Cream Ingredients

1 cup vegan sour cream

2 tablespoons fresh lemon juice

1 teaspoon agave nectar

2 tablespoons fresh dill, finely chopped

½ teaspoon sea salt

½ teaspoon finely ground black pepper

Guacamole Ingredients

1 ripe avocado

2 tablespoons fresh lime juice (about ½ lime)

¼ teaspoon sea salt, plus to taste

¼ teaspoon finely ground black pepper

1 tablespoon red onion, finely chopped

Remaining Ingredients

1 (15-ounce) can pinto beans, rinsed

½ teaspoon sea salt

¼ teaspoon ground chipotle pepper

2 teaspoons neutral tasting oil

2 teaspoons red wine vinegar

1 large bag unsalted corn tortilla chips

4 scallions (green onions), sliced into thin rounds

10-12 black pitted olives, sliced into rounds

Directions

For the cashew cheese: Heat a medium (4-quart) pot. Add almond or soymilk. When warm, add agar agar flakes and bring to a simmer. Cook mixture over low-medium heat for about 15 minutes, stirring occasionally, or until agar agar is mostly dissolved. Set aside.

In a food processor or high-powered blender, add cashews, garlic powder, sea salt, paprika, miso, nutritional yeast, agave, oil and lemon juice. If using a high-powered blender, put in dry ingredients and almond or soymilk mixture all at once. If using a food processor, add dry ingredients first, pulse about 10-15 times, then add almond or soymilk mixture, blending until smooth and uniform. Mixture can be cooled and reheated to melt.

(continued on next page)

Nachos with a Melty Cashew Cheese, Lemon Herb Sour Cream and Guacamole (gf)

(continued from previous page)

Directions (continued)

For the lemon herb sour cream:
Whisk together sour cream, lemon juice, agave, dill, sea salt and black pepper. Set aside to develop flavors for 15 minutes.

For the guacamole: Peel avocado and dice, placing in a large bowl. Add lime juice, sea salt and black pepper. Mash with a fork until creamy. Fold in red onion and set aside.

In a small (2-quart) pot over medium heat, add beans, sea salt, chipotle pepper, oil and vinegar, and heat until cooked through. Remove from heat.

To assemble: Place a layer of chips on a large platter or individual small plates. Spread beans evenly over chips. Add another layer of chips and pour a layer of melted cashew cheese. Top with guacamole, scallions and olives. Drizzle with lemon herb sour cream. Serve immediately.

The Sporkie Scoop

FOR YOUR SMARTS Agar agar (a.k.a. agar) is an amazing seaweed used to thicken sauces and is 5 times stronger than gelatin! Not only does it possess tons of minerals and amino acids, but because it grows in the ocean under a lot of pressure and battling the currents, it develops powerful polysaccharides, which are used in gums for all types of cooking and scientific purposes.

FOR YOUR PARTS Eating dill is a great idea after a night of heavy drinking. It helps detox your liver, ridding it of toxic chemicals — or a stiff dirty martini.[6]

Spiced Beer-Soaked Figs with a Ricotta Filling

Make these when figs are in season, which is usually from May to October, depending on the variety. Whether you are having a fancy-shmancy dinner or just enjoying a simple meal at home with your loved ones, these beautiful stuffed figs will be a perfect addition to your din din. If you have some extra ricotta filling handy, you can use it to stuff manicotti! **Serves 6-8**

Ricotta Ingredients

1 cup cashews

1 tablespoon light miso paste

½ cup water

1 (14-ounce) block extra-firm tofu, crumbled (see recipe for homemade tofu on p. 84)

½-1 teaspoon sea salt

¼ teaspoon finely ground black pepper

½ teaspoon garlic powder

3 tablespoons fresh lemon juice

2 teaspoons agave nectar

Dash freshly grated nutmeg

2 tablespoons extra-virgin olive oil

Fig Ingredients

1 pint vegan beer

8-10 whole cloves

½ teaspoon sea salt

¼ teaspoon finely ground black pepper

2 teaspoons agave nectar

2 teaspoons fresh lemon juice

24 fresh figs (Calimyrna preferred)

6-8 leaves fresh basil or sage, for garnish (optional)

Directions

For the ricotta: In a blender or food processor, add cashews, miso and water. Blend until smooth and set aside.

In a large bowl, combine crumbled tofu, sea salt, black pepper, garlic powder, lemon juice, agave, nutmeg, olive oil and the cashew mixture.

Mix together well. Set aside for 20-30 minutes to develop flavors.

For the beer-soaked figs: In a medium (4-quart) pot, bring beer to a simmer over medium heat. Add cloves, sea salt, black pepper, agave and lemon juice.

Continue cooking over low heat for about 3 minutes, or until fragrant.

Slice off stems of figs and make 2 cuts on top of fig in a T shape; this is where filling will go. (When cooking, figs will open slightly.) When cut, place all figs in pot with beer mixture and cook over low-medium heat for about 5-7 minutes. Turn off heat and let figs rest in spiced beer for additional 3-5 minutes.

To assemble: Place 1 tablespoon ricotta filling in each fig and serve on a platter. Garnish with fresh basil or sage, if using.

The Sporkie Scoop

FOR YOUR SMARTS There are over 150 varieties of figs in this big world. Some of the most popular include Calimyrna, Kadota, Black Mission, Brown Turkey and Adriatic. Our fave for this recipe is Calimyrna!

FOR YOUR PARTS Olive oil contains vitamin E, which is a natural preservative and prevents these beautifully rich oils from spoiling! Extra-virgin has the most nutritional value and is the least processed.

Spanakopita with Homemade Tofu Feta

We take a sister trip each year to see the world, make new friends and most importantly, eat things we've never tried or even heard of. One of our fave trips was to Greece, where we sat on the beaches of Crete, Santorini and Mykonos, drinking white wine and eating spanakopita. We relive our trip every time we make this Greek snack, and it will take you away on a vacay too!

Yields about 10-12 pieces

Ingredients

2 tablespoons neutral tasting high-heat oil

1 teaspoon dried oregano

1 (14-ounce) block extra-firm tofu, crumbled (see recipe for homemade tofu on p. 84)

5 cloves roasted garlic (see roasting directions on p. 2)

½ teaspoon sea salt

½ teaspoon finely ground black pepper

2 tablespoons light miso paste

2 tablespoons red wine vinegar

2 tablespoons fresh lemon juice, plus grated zest of 1 lemon

1 tablespoon brown rice syrup

1 tablespoon fresh thyme

4 cups spinach, tightly packed

1 package frozen puff pastry sheets, thawed

1 tablespoon sesame seeds (optional)

Directions

Preheat oven to 400°F.

In a large pan, combine oil, oregano and crumbled tofu. Add roasted garlic, sea salt, black pepper, miso, vinegar, lemon juice and zest, brown rice syrup and thyme. Cook for about 5-7 minutes, stirring occasionally, until tofu appears slightly dry and golden.

Add spinach to tofu mixture in small bunches and cook until wilted. Remove excess water once cooked.

To assemble: Slice each sheet of thawed puff pastry into 4-inch squares. Add about 2 tablespoons filling to upper left corner of each square. Fold puff pastry in half over filling to create a triangle.

Seal edges by pressing with a fork.

Make 2 small slits in the top of spanakopita. Repeat for remaining puff pastry. Top with sesame seeds, if using.

Place on a large baking sheet, lined with parchment paper or a silicone baking mat (or use cooking spray). Bake for about 20 minutes, or until crisp and golden.

The Sporkie Scoop

FOR YOUR SMARTS Tofu has a high calcium content, so there are better ways to build strong bones than consuming cow's milk—and that's the truth!

FOR YOUR PARTS Miso, like other fermented foods, contains lactobacillus, a beneficial bacterium that can fight off unfriendly bacteria in your intestines![7]

Beer-Battered Tempeh Fish with a Tartar Sauce

These golden beauties are crunchy on the outside but soft and delicate on the inside! They go well with your favorite pint of vegan ale (we would personally choose a full-bodied pale ale). Cheers! **Serves 4-6**

Tempeh Fish Ingredients

2 cups unbleached all-purpose flour

1 tablespoon non-aluminum baking powder

1 teaspoon sea salt, plus ½ teaspoon

¼ teaspoon finely ground black pepper

¼ teaspoon cayenne pepper, plus ¼ teaspoon

¼ teaspoon garlic powder

1 (16-ounce) bottle pale ale, cold

Water for steaming

2 packages soy tempeh, sliced into 1-inch-thick strips

¼ cup malt vinegar

2 tablespoons agave nectar

3 cups neutral tasting high-heat oil

Tartar Sauce Ingredients

1 cup vegan mayonnaise

1 tablespoon pickle relish

4 green pimiento-stuffed olives, finely chopped

1 tablespoon non-pareil (small) capers, drained

1 teaspoon dried minced onion

1 tablespoon fresh lemon juice

¼ teaspoon sea salt

¼ teaspoon cayenne pepper

Directions

In a large bowl, whisk together flour, baking powder, 1 teaspoon sea salt, black pepper, ¼ teaspoon cayenne pepper, and garlic powder. Slowly whisk in beer until batter is smooth and uniform. Refrigerate for 15 minutes to relax the gluten.

Meanwhile, fill a large (6-quart) pot with about 1 inch of water and place a steamer basket in the pot. Bring to a simmer with lid on. Place tempeh strips in steamer basket, cover and steam over low heat for about 5 minutes. This removes any bitter flavor the tempeh may have. Allow to cool slightly. Place tempeh strips in a bowl and coat with malt vinegar, agave, remaining sea salt and cayenne. Set aside.

Heat a medium (4-quart) pot and add oil. Heat for about 4 minutes over high heat. To test for optimal frying temperature, insert a clean wooden cooking tool. When bubbles form around base of tool, add battered tempeh.

(continued on next page)

Beer-Battered Tempeh Fish with a Tartar Sauce

(continued from previous page)

Directions (continued)

Alternatively, heat oil to 325°F on a deep-fry thermometer.

Dip tempeh into beer batter, then carefully place into hot oil with tongs, slowly submerging tempeh. When golden on one side, turn over and cook until golden on remaining side, about 2 minutes. Drain on paper towels.

For the tartar sauce: Whisk mayonnaise, pickle relish, olives, capers, minced onion, lemon juice, sea salt and cayenne in a small bowl. Set aside.

Serve warm tempeh fish with tartar sauce and malt vinegar on the side.

Note: Tony Yanow (from Tony's Darts Away, our FAVE pub in Burbank, CA) recommends using a Firestone Walker Pale 31 for the beer batter.

The Sporkie Scoop

FOR YOUR SMARTS Malt comes from sprouted and dried grains (usually barley) that are then ground into a powder and used not only for malt vinegar, but also to distill liquor and brew beer. So you can see why it goes so well with these beer-battered beauties.

FOR YOUR PARTS Cayenne is a spicy red chili pepper that has incredible amounts of healing powers! This little sucka prevents stomach ulcers, promotes digestion and rebuilds the stomach lining. Tummies and cayenne are lovers in disguise.[8]

SOUPS & SALADS

*(gf) indicates the recipe is gluten-free!

Caribbean Salad with Crispy Plantains and Avocado Mango Salsa in a Light Lemon Vinaigrette (gf)

If you're looking for a summertime salad to take your taste buds on a vacay, look no further! The combination of crispy plantains, avo mango salsa, hearts of palm, cashews and some greens makes this meal of a salad well worth the little bit of effort. It doesn't hurt to set the mood with some Bob Marley in the background. **Serves 4-6**

Salad Ingredients

3 cups (loosely packed) baby lettuce or mixed lettuce greens, washed and roughly chopped

¼ cup cashews

½ cup hearts of palm, cut into rounds

Plantain Ingredients

⅓ cup neutral tasting high-heat oil

2 large green plantains, sliced into ¼-inch-thick rounds

½ teaspoon garlic powder

¼ teaspoon sea salt

2 tablespoons fresh lime juice

1 tablespoon agave nectar

Dressing Ingredients

¼ cup extra-virgin olive oil

2 teaspoons agave nectar

2 tablespoons fresh lemon juice

1 tablespoon mustard, stone ground or German

½ teaspoon sea salt

¼ teaspoon finely ground black pepper

Avocado Mango Salsa Ingredients

1 ripe mango, peeled and diced

1 large ripe avocado

1 tablespoon fresh lime juice

½ teaspoon sea salt

½ teaspoon finely ground black pepper

1 tablespoon red onion, finely chopped

1 tablespoon neutral tasting oil

1 teaspoon hot sauce (or mango pepper sauce)

Directions

Place salad greens in a large bowl with enough room to toss with dressing, and set aside.

Toast cashews on a baking sheet at 375°F for about 5 minutes. Set aside.

For the plantains: Heat a large sauté pan and add oil. Over medium-high heat, add plantains, garlic powder and sea salt. Cook on each side for about 3 minutes, or until well browned. Remove from heat and place on a plate lined with a paper towel. Drizzle with lime juice and agave and set aside.

For the dressing: Place olive oil, agave, lemon juice, mustard, sea salt and black pepper in a blender or food processor. Blend until dressing is creamy and uniform.

For the salsa: Place diced mango in a large bowl. Peel and dice avocado and add to bowl. Add lime juice, sea salt, black pepper, onion, oil and hot sauce. Set aside, allowing flavors to develop.

To assemble the salad, add sliced hearts of palm and cashews to salad greens. Toss together with dressing. Top salad with plantains and salsa.

The Sporkie Scoop

FOR YOUR SMARTS Plantains are bananas best used for cooking because they remain dry and starch-like, never converting their starches to sugars the same way as sweet bananas. Botanically speaking, a banana is a berry, along with eggplant, grapes and watermelon!

FOR YOUR PARTS No need for smack-talking about avo's high fat content. Their oils are insanely good for you and can bring your bad cholesterol levels (LDL) down and good ones (HDL) up![9]

Amazing Caesar Salad with Homemade Croutons

It's amazing how a dressing that traditionally depends so heavily on eggs and anchovies can be so easily veganized! This dressing is great on a salad, of course, but don't stop there! Try using some in a wrap or as a dip for veggies. You can even use a little on the corn cake appetizers from p. 10, instead of the smoky paprika sauce, for a bit of variation. **Serves 6-8**

Salad Ingredients

2-3 heads romaine lettuce, washed and roughly chopped

2 tablespoons non-pareil (small) capers, drained

Dressing Ingredients

⅓ cup vegan mayonnaise

1 teaspoon brown rice syrup

1 tablespoon vegan Worcestershire sauce

2 tablespoons fresh lemon juice

5 cloves roasted garlic (see roasting directions on p. 2)

¼ cup toasted walnuts

¼ cup toasted almonds

2 teaspoons nutritional yeast flakes

2 teaspoons light miso paste

½ teaspoon sea salt

¼ teaspoon finely ground black pepper

Homemade Crouton Ingredients

4 slices spelt bread

1 tablespoon neutral tasting high-heat oil

1 teaspoon brown rice syrup

¼ teaspoon sea salt

Crouton Ingredients (continued)

¼ teaspoon finely ground black pepper

½ teaspoon paprika

¼ teaspoon chili powder

¼ teaspoon garlic powder

½ teaspoon dried oregano

Directions

Place salad greens in a large bowl with enough room to toss with dressing.

For the dressing: Place mayonnaise, brown rice syrup, Worcestershire sauce, lemon juice, garlic, walnuts, almonds, nutritional yeast, miso, sea salt and black pepper in a food processor or high-powered blender. Blend until dressing is creamy and uniform. Set aside in refrigerator until ready to use. Refrigerate for about 30 minutes to let flavors develop.

For the croutons: Preheat oven to 375°F.

Cut bread into small cubes and place in a bowl. Add oil, brown rice syrup, sea salt, black pepper, paprika, chili powder, garlic powder and oregano. Toss to coat.

Place bread cubes on an ungreased, rimmed baking sheet and bake for about 10-12 minutes, or until croutons are crisp. Let cool before using.

To serve, toss salad greens with dressing. Top with croutons and capers.

Note: Croutons can keep for up to 1 week in an airtight container or metal tin.

The Sporkie Scoop

FOR YOUR SMARTS Rumor has it, the Caesar salad was created in Tijuana in 1924 by a man named Caesar Cardini, who lived in San Diego but owned a restaurant in Mexico to get around Prohibition.

FOR YOUR PARTS Capers are an edible flower, eaten long before they bloom! They're good for you and crazy high in cancer-fighting antioxidants!

Velvety Carrot Soup with Mint Oil (gf)

Heavy whipping cream is the go-to source for some creamy soups, but whoa … is it gnarly for the bod! One cup of heavy cream can have a whopping 88 grams of fat, and 326 milligrams of cholesterol. Yep. We prefer to use a potato to thicken our soup and make it creamy, because it totally does the trick and has zilch fat and cholesterol. Drizzling this soup with the mint oil adds a little fresh flavor and sophistication. To be classy about it, try serving this soup as soup shooters for your next par-tay. **Serves 4-6**

Soup Ingredients

2 tablespoons non-dairy butter

1 medium onion, finely chopped

3 cloves garlic, finely chopped

6 large carrots, roughly chopped

4 cups vegetable broth (low-sodium)

1 cup vegan white wine,
or 1 additional cup vegetable broth

1 large organic russet potato,
diced (about ½ cup)

¾ teaspoon sea salt

½ teaspoon finely ground
black pepper

1 bay leaf

1 tablespoon agave nectar

1 tablespoon fresh lemon juice,
plus grated zest of 1 lemon

2 tablespoons unsweetened almond
or soymilk or coconut milk creamer

Mint Oil Ingredients

22-25 leaves fresh mint
(about 5 sprigs), chopped

¼ cup extra-virgin olive oil

¼ cup neutral tasting oil

½ teaspoon fresh lemon juice

¼ teaspoon sea salt

Directions

Preheat a large (6-quart) pot. Add butter and sauté onion and garlic over medium heat for about 2 minutes, until slightly browned. Add carrots and cook for 2 more minutes.

Add vegetable broth, white wine, potato, sea salt, black pepper and bay leaf.

Reduce heat to a simmer and cook, partially covered, for about 20 minutes, or until carrots are very tender. Remove bay leaf and add agave, lemon juice and zest, and almond or soymilk or creamer.

Transfer to a blender. Remove center of lid to allow heat to escape. Blend soup until smooth and creamy. Transfer back to cooking pot to reheat.

For the mint oil: Blend mint leaves, olive oil, neutral oil, lemon juice and sea salt in food processor or blender. Strain through a fine mesh strainer, reserving mint oil in a bowl.

To serve soup, ladle into serving bowls and drizzle 2 teaspoons mint oil in a spiral pattern over center of each bowl.

The Sporkie Scoop

FOR YOUR SMARTS Mint has deep roots in Greek mythology! Hades (ruler of the underworld) fell in love with a nymph named Menthe (who lends her name to the menthol oil in mint) and his wife got pissed, of course! To appease her, Hades transformed Menthe into a shrub, making wifey happy because she thought everyone would just trample her. However, Hades got to enjoy her scent anytime he passed by this sweet shrub.[10]

FOR YOUR PARTS Bay leaves do more than just flavor food! Want a home remedy for dandruff? Steep crushed bay leaves in boiling water for 20 minutes, cool, strain and pour the liquid on your head. Wrap your head in a towel for an hour and then rinse it out! The anti-fungal and anti-microbial properties in this powerful leaf will fight the druff and get you back to your normal, gorgeous self.

French Onion Soup with a Cheesy Crouton Topping

This classic French delicacy has been around for hundreds of years. It began as a way to use an inexpensive ingredient, onions, to fill up the bod, but later became a regal dish full of cheese and other artery-cloggers. French onion soup is best served in individual ramekins or cocottes, to fit the crunchy crouton topping (our recipe uses a simpler version of the traditional croutons, keeping all the crouton crunch). If you don't have ramekins, now is the time to invest, because this soup is worth it!

Serves 6-8

Ingredients

2 tablespoons non-dairy butter

3 medium brown onions, thinly sliced

2 cloves garlic, finely chopped

5 cups vegetable broth (low-sodium)

¼ cup vegan red wine

1 tablespoon light miso paste

1 cup toasted walnuts, roughly chopped

½ teaspoon sea salt

½ teaspoon finely ground black pepper

1 bay leaf

1 tablespoon fresh lemon juice

2 sprigs fresh thyme, finely chopped

1 organic French baguette

1 cup shredded vegan cheese

Directions

Preheat a large (6-quart) pot. Add butter and sauté onions and garlic over low heat for about 7-10 minutes. Add vegetable broth, red wine, miso, walnuts, sea salt, black pepper, bay leaf, lemon juice and thyme.

Cook partially covered for about 20 minutes at a simmer, or until onions are very tender.

Turn on broiler (high setting preferred).

Slice baguette into 1-inch-thick rounds and set aside.

Ladle soup into heat-tolerant ramekins or cocottes. Place one round of bread on each serving of soup and top with about 2 tablespoons cheese. Place ramekins on a large baking dish with sides and broil for about 2 minutes, or until cheese on top of soup is bubbling.

Serve on an appetizer plate, because ramekins will be very hot!

Note: One container of veggie broth usually has 4 cups, so buy 2 containers if making this recipe! Also, not all red wine is animal-friendly, so to find out if your fave wine is vegan, visit www.barnivore.com, or call the winemaker and ask!

The Sporkie Scoop

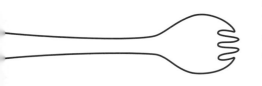

FOR YOUR SMARTS Veggie broth is easy to make on your own if you have the time! Take your sturdiest pot, fill it with water and throw in roughly chopped fresh carrots, celery and onion from the farmer's market. Spice it up with some garlic and peppercorns or jazz it up with other spices—anything goes. Boil for about 30 mins, strain your veggies and done, done, done. This is a great excuse to practice your cutting techniques!

FOR YOUR PARTS Eating onions can help prevent bone loss, similar to the ways that certain pharmaceutical drugs can![11]

Green Salad with Creamy Tempeh Bacon Ranch Dressing

Some restaurants think that all a vegan needs is a plain salad with a balsamic vinaigrette. Snoresville. We know that there's more to vegan dressing than that—and we love pushing the envelope! Put this tempeh bacon ranch over salad or use it as a dip for veggies. It doesn't hurt a baked potato either. Just sayin'. **Yields 1 cup dressing. Serves 4-6**

Salad Ingredients

3 cups (loosely packed) baby greens or romaine lettuce, washed and roughly chopped

3 red radishes, sliced into thin rounds

Tempeh Bacon Ingredients

1 tablespoon non-dairy butter or refined coconut oil

1 package tempeh bacon, finely chopped

1 clove garlic, finely chopped

¼ teaspoon finely ground black pepper

Dressing Ingredients

¾ cup vegan mayonnaise

3 tablespoons unsweetened almond or soymilk, curdled with ½ teaspoon unfiltered apple cider vinegar

1 tablespoon maple syrup

Dressing ingredients (continued)

½ teaspoon vegan Worcestershire sauce

1 tablespoon fresh lemon or lime juice

¼ teaspoon garlic powder

1 teaspoon dried minced onion

¼ teaspoon celery seeds

¼ teaspoon sea salt

¼ teaspoon finely ground black pepper

Directions

Place salad greens in a large bowl. Set aside.

For the tempeh bacon: Heat a large sauté pan and add butter or coconut oil. Add chopped tempeh bacon, garlic and black pepper. Sauté over medium heat for about 3 minutes, or until browned.

For the dressing: In a bowl, combine mayonnaise, curdled almond or soymilk, maple syrup, Worcestershire sauce, lemon or lime juice, garlic powder, minced onion, celery seeds, sea salt and black pepper. Whisk to incorporate. Add cooked tempeh bacon and mix in thoroughly.

To serve, toss salad greens and radish slices with dressing.

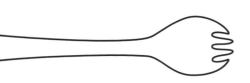

The Sporkie Scoop

FOR YOUR SMARTS Radishes haven't always been rosy. They were first cultivated in Egypt over 4,000 years ago and were originally black.

FOR YOUR PARTS Celery seeds have a ton of health benefits! In alternative medicine they're used to treat symptoms of gout, stimulate blood flow, and act as a diuretic—but our fave fact is that they help with sleeplessness and anxiety. Nighty night![12]

Chilled Creamy Red and Yellow Gazpacho

This pure and simple soup is a pleasure to make because you only need a blender! It's the ultimate soup for a hot day when you don't feel like breaking a sweat in the kitch. You can make the red or yellow gazpacho by itself, but there is nothing more impressive than two soups in one bowl. Seriously ... look at that pic. **Serves 4-6**

Red Gazpacho Ingredients

6-8 grape tomatoes, halved

1 large red heirloom tomato, roughly chopped

½ large red bell pepper, roughly chopped

1 clove fresh or roasted garlic, finely chopped (see roasting directions on p. 2)

2 tablespoons red onion, finely chopped

2 slices whole wheat bread

½ teaspoon red wine vinegar or sherry vinegar

½ teaspoon Champagne vinegar

½ teaspoon sea salt

½ teaspoon finely ground black pepper

3 tablespoons extra-virgin olive oil

1 cup Persian or English cucumber, finely chopped

⅓ cup toasted Marcona almonds, for garnish (optional)

Yellow Gazpacho Ingredients

15-18 yellow pear tomatoes, halved

1 large yellow heirloom tomato, roughly chopped

½ large yellow bell pepper, roughly chopped

1 clove fresh or roasted garlic, finely chopped (see roasting directions on p. 2)

2 slices whole wheat bread

5-8 strands saffron

3 tablespoons fresh lemon juice, plus grated zest of 1 lemon

½ teaspoon Champagne vinegar

½ teaspoon sea salt

½ teaspoon finely ground black pepper

3 tablespoons extra-virgin olive oil

Directions

For the red gazpacho: Place tomatoes, bell pepper, garlic, onion and bread in a blender or food processor, Add red wine or sherry vinegar, Champagne vinegar, sea salt, black pepper and olive oil.

Blend mixture until smooth and creamy, about 30-60 seconds. Remove from blender or food processor; refrigerate for 30 minutes to overnight.

For the yellow gazpacho: Place tomatoes, bell pepper, garlic and bread in a blender or food processor. Add saffron, lemon juice and zest, Champagne vinegar, sea salt, black pepper and olive oil.

(continued on next page)

Chilled Creamy Red and Yellow Gazpacho

(continued from previous page)

Directions (continued)

Blend mixture until smooth and creamy, about 30-60 seconds. Remove from blender or food processor; refrigerate for 30 minutes to overnight.

To serve, pour red gazpacho and yellow gazpacho into separate pitchers that have large spouts. Using both pitchers at the same time, carefully pour red and yellow gazpacho, side by side, into the same soup bowl. Top with cucumbers, or for crunch, garnish with toasted Marcona almonds, if using.

Note for both soups: The longer gazpacho sits, the more pronounced its flavors will be.

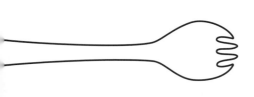

The Sporkie Scoop

FOR YOUR SMARTS   Conventional bell peps are treated heavily with pesticides, so let's go organic on these, for surezies.

FOR YOUR PARTS   Tomatoes are packed with nutrients, water and antioxidants. Why do we care? Because this combo plate can actually help protect our sexy selves from the damaging effects of the sun![13]

Southwest Chopped Salad with Grilled Corn and Tortilla Strips in a Creamy Basil Dressing

We're not dainty ladies who get full from eating a side salad. We like our salads over-the-top and packed with the goods because we often eat one as a meal, so we want it to have some texture and color. We do have to admit, there is beauty in simplicity—but salad is not the time to show it. **Serves 4-6**

Salad Ingredients

3 cups romaine lettuce, washed and roughly chopped

2 whole grain spelt tortillas

1 tablespoon neutral tasting oil

¼ teaspoon sea salt, plus dash

¼ teaspoon finely ground black pepper, plus dash

2 tablespoons fresh lime juice

1 teaspoon non-dairy butter

1 ear fresh corn, kernels sliced from cob

½ teaspoon dried basil

½ large English cucumber, diced

1 medium heirloom tomato, diced

Creamy Basil Dressing Ingredients

15-17 leaves fresh basil, finely chopped

1 tablespoon extra-virgin olive oil

½ teaspoon sea salt

½ teaspoon finely ground black pepper

2 tablespoons fresh lemon juice

2 tablespoons brown rice syrup

¾ cup vegan mayonnaise

Directions

Place salad greens in a large bowl. Set aside.

For the tortilla strips: Preheat oven to 375°F.

Cut tortillas into small strips and place on a rimmed baking sheet. Add oil, sea salt, black pepper and lime juice, and toss together to coat. Spread strips out evenly.

Bake for about 8-10 minutes, or until strips are crisp. Let cool and set aside.

For the grilled corn: Heat a sauté pan over medium heat and add butter. Add corn, basil, and a dash each of sea salt and black pepper, and cook until the corn looks slightly golden. Set aside.

For the dressing: Combine basil, olive oil, sea salt, black pepper, lemon juice, brown rice syrup and mayonnaise in a bowl and whisk until uniform.

To serve, toss salad greens with dressing. Top with cucumber, tomato, and grilled corn, and garnish with tortilla strips.

Note: Tortilla strips can keep for up to 1 week in an airtight container or metal tin.

The Sporkie Scoop

FOR YOUR SMARTS One of our fave tricks for weight loss involves cucumbers! At only 14 calories a cup, cucumber rounds are a great way to scoop and eat our assorted dips, instead of crackers or bread.

FOR YOUR PARTS Two cups of romaine lettuce is only 16 calories and romaine is packed with more nutrients than most varieties of lettuce![14]

Niçoise Salad

Just saying Niçoise (knee-swahz) makes you sound like you know what you're talking about. This delightful (loosely) French recipe is perfect for a sophisticated din din. You can create a beautiful presentation with all the ingredients, but just remember to warn your guests if you use olives with pits! **Serves 4-6**

Salad Ingredients

2 heads red leaf or butter lettuce, washed and roughly chopped

4 quarts water for boiling

Dash sea salt

4-5 small organic new red potatoes, quartered

1 cup green beans, trimmed and cut into 1-inch pieces

½ package baked tofu, diced (about 1 cup)

½ cup Niçoise olives

½ large avocado, diced

Dressing Ingredients

¼ cup fresh lemon juice

1 tablespoon red wine vinegar (Cabernet preferred)

½ cup extra-virgin olive oil

1 large shallot, finely diced

4 sprigs fresh thyme, stemmed and chopped

3-5 sprigs fresh oregano, stemmed and chopped

½ teaspoon dried basil

2 teaspoons mustard, stone ground or German

Dressing Ingredients (continued)

2 tablespoons brown rice syrup

¼ teaspoon sea salt

¼ teaspoon finely ground black pepper

Directions

Place salad greens in a large bowl and set aside.

For the dressing: In blender or food processor, combine lemon juice, vinegar, olive oil, shallot, thyme, oregano, basil, mustard, brown rice syrup, and sea salt and black pepper, and blend until uniform and creamy. Set aside.

Bring water and sea salt to a boil in a large (6-quart) pot. Add potatoes and cook until tender, about 8-10 minutes. Using a slotted spoon, remove potatoes from water and place in a bowl.

Keep boiling water going and add a dash more sea salt.

Add cut green beans and cook for 1-2 minutes, or until they float to top and turn bright green. Drain and submerge green beans in cold water. Drain again and place in a bowl.

Coat potatoes with about 3 tablespoons dressing and set aside. Coat cooled green beans with about 2 tablespoons dressing and set aside.

Toss salad greens with remaining dressing until well coated.

Arrange toppings in bunches, starting with potatoes, followed by green beans, baked tofu, Niçoise olives and avocado.

Note: If you are having a hard time finding Niçoise olives, you can use Kalamata olives!

The Sporkie Scoop

FOR YOUR SMARTS The Niçoise salad is named after the French city of Nice, located on the southern Mediterranean coast. This dish was just made to be veganized because of the potential of the assorted fresh veggies and beautiful olive oil. We can do without traditional ingredients like hard-boiled egg, tuna and anchovies!

FOR YOUR PARTS Olives have anti-inflammatory properties that can help with asthma and arthritis symptoms![15]

Creamy Tomato Soup

When we picture our grandpa going off to work in the 1950s with a thermos in tow, we know he had some creamy tomato soup in there. Whether or not it was vegan is a different story. Because we use real tomatoes and a potato to thicken this recipe, it's much healthier than the modern stuff you get in a can. When you're in the mood for a comforting recipe that doesn't take too long to create, try this soup! **Serves 6**

Ingredients

2 tablespoons non-dairy butter

1 tablespoon whole wheat pastry flour

1 medium onion, finely chopped

2 cloves garlic, finely chopped

2 cups fresh cherry tomatoes

1 (15-ounce) can diced tomatoes

4 cups vegetable broth (low-sodium)

1 large organic russet potato, diced

¾ teaspoon sea salt, plus to taste

½ teaspoon finely ground black pepper, plus to taste

½ teaspoon ground cinnamon

1 tablespoon fresh lemon juice

1 tablespoon agave nectar

. ¼ cup soy creamer

Croutons for topping (optional) — see recipe for homemade croutons on p. 28

Directions

Preheat a large (6-quart) pot. Add butter, flour, onion and garlic, and sauté over medium heat for about 3-4 minutes, or until slightly browned. Add fresh and canned tomatoes and cook for 2 more minutes.

Add vegetable broth, potato, sea salt, black pepper and cinnamon. Reduce heat to a simmer and cook, partially covered, for about 20 minutes, or until potatoes are very tender. Add lemon juice, agave and creamer.

Blend soup with immersion blender, or in a blender with middle section of lid removed. If using a blender, place a dish towel over top of blender to prevent spillage. Season to taste with sea salt and black pepper. Serve warm and top with croutons if using.

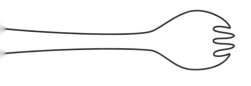

The Sporkie Scoop

FOR YOUR SMARTS   Tomatoes are a fruit, botanically speaking. Back in the day, there were tariffs for veggies, but not fruits, which caused an uproar. The United States Supreme Court took the issue into its own hands, and in 1893 declared that the tomato was a vegetable, and therefore subject to taxation.

FOR YOUR PARTS   Black pepper has been popular for a very long time, and it's still not out of style! Not only was it used for ages to spice up bland foods, but it also covered up flavors of spoiled foods before people were lucky enough to have refrigerators. This good stuff may also help break down fat cells![16]

Jerk Coleslaw with Plantain Strips (gf)

One of the best parts about traveling, in our humble opinion, is tasting new foods! When Jenny traveled to Jamaica, she loved trying traditional Rastafarian Ital food — fresh coconuts, and plantains galore. But the one dish no one had veganized was the jerk coleslaw. We had to get to work creating our own version when she got back. We've been told it's very authentic and delish, with a little vegan West Hollywood spin! **Serves 6-8**

Ingredients

½ large head purple cabbage
½ large head green cabbage

Dressing Ingredients

3 cloves roasted garlic
(for roasting directions see p. 2)
1 cup vegan mayonnaise
2 tablespoons fresh lime juice,
plus grated zest of 1 lime
2 teaspoons fresh chives,
finely chopped
2 heaping teaspoons
jerk seasoning blend
½ teaspoon sea salt,
plus to taste
½ teaspoon finely ground
black pepper, plus to taste

Plantain Strip Ingredients

2 tablespoons neutral
tasting high-heat oil
1 large green plantain
Dash garlic powder

Directions

Slice purple cabbage in half. Shred by placing flat portion on cutting board. Make even, small slices into cabbage until well chopped. Repeat for green cabbage. Place in a medium bowl and set aside.

For the dressing: Chop garlic and place in a medium bowl. Add mayonnaise, lime juice and zest, chives, jerk seasoning, sea salt and black pepper. Whisk until uniform.

For the plaintain strips: Heat a sauté pan and add oil. Remove plantain from peel. Using a peeler, make long strips lengthwise along plantain. Add strips to oil and cook for about 2 minutes on each side, or until crisp. Place on a plate lined with a paper towel. Season to taste with sea salt, black pepper and garlic powder.

Toss cabbage with dressing until well coated. To serve, top with plantain strips.

Note: Shred cabbage quickly in a food processor using the slicing blade attachment.

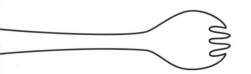

The Sporkie Scoop

FOR YOUR SMARTS Ital food gets its name from the word "vital" and represents the Rastafarian diet. Many Rastafarians are vegan and emphasize using pure, unprocessed ingredients to promote "Livity," or life energy. We feel this!

FOR YOUR PARTS Have you ever heard of vitamin U? We didn't make it up. This vitey is found in cabbage and may actually help heal ulcers! Though it may not be delish, juicing cabbage is effective for treating certain stomach ulcers.[17]

SIDES

SIDES

*(gf) indicates the recipe is gluten-free!

Spicy Corn Fritters with Lemongrass (gf)

These lil' fritters are special! They get a lot of their essence from lemongrass, one of the most important flavors of Thai and Vietnamese cuisine. Just the smell of these fritters cooking will attract attention from neighbors all around. When you make a Southeast Asian feast, be sure these are part of the menu. **Yields 8 fritters**

Ingredients

⅔ cup gluten-free cornmeal, plus ½ cup for coating

3 tablespoons rice flour

2 teaspoons non-aluminum baking powder

2 tablespoons maple syrup

1 tablespoon neutral tasting high-heat oil

2 tablespoons fresh lime juice

1 tablespoon tamari (wheat-free)

1 tablespoon chili paste (chili garlic paste or sweet chili paste)

2 teaspoons finely grated fresh ginger

½ teaspoon sea salt

1 ear corn, kernels sliced from cob, or ⅓ cup frozen corn kernels

½ stalk lemongrass, finely chopped

¼ cup water, more or less, as needed

⅓ cup neutral tasting high-heat oil

Directions

In a medium bowl, combine ⅔ cup cornmeal, rice flour and baking powder. Whisk until uniform.

Add maple syrup, oil, lime juice, tamari, chili paste, ginger and sea salt, and whisk.

Add corn, lemongrass and water to mixture. Amount of water needed will vary, depending on which brand of rice flour is used. Consistency should be fairly firm and mixture should hold together when scooped. Form mixture into 2-inch round patties.

Add additional cornmeal to a bowl and coat patties. Tap patties gently to remove excess cornmeal.

Heat a large sauté pan and add high-heat oil. Place patties in pan and cook over low-medium heat for about 3-5 minutes on each side, until golden.

Note: You can double the recipe when serving more than four.

The Sporkie Scoop

FOR YOUR SMARTS Lemongrass is native to Southeast Asia and has been consumed and used as medicine for thousands of years! Lemongrass is a general term for about 55 species of grasses. Some types are used in perfumes and cosmetics because of the clean, fresh smell.[18]

FOR YOUR PARTS Lime juice contains a compound called limonene, which is a major cancer fighter! It can also boost your white blood cell activity. That's some powerful citrus![19]

Patatas Bravas (Spiced Baby Potatoes) (gf)

We love hosting tapas-themed cooking classes because there is something about tapas that says insta-party. Maybe it's the sangria or the idea that these foods are supposed to be accompanied by wine, but whatever the case—it's a good time! These spiced potatoes can be served as a side dish, as an appetizer with cute frilly toothpicks, or, of course, served tapas-style—as a small plate with a variety of other appies. **Serves 6-8 as an appetizer, 3-4 as a side dish**

Ingredients

2-3 cups small, organic fingerling or new potatoes

2 tablespoons neutral tasting high-heat oil

¼ teaspoon sea salt, plus to taste

¼ teaspoon finely ground black pepper, plus to taste

½ teaspoon dried thyme

1 tablespoon smoked paprika

¼ teaspoon chili powder

1 clove garlic, finely chopped

1 tablespoon fresh thyme, finely chopped

½ cup ketchup

¼ cup vegan mayonnaise

½ cup microgreens, for garnish (optional)

Directions

Preheat oven to 375°F.

Place potatoes on a baking sheet and coat them in oil, sea salt, black pepper and thyme.

Bake for about 20-25 minutes, stirring once halfway through. Bake until skins are brown and potatoes give little resistance when poked with a fork.

Meanwhile, in a mixing bowl, whisk together paprika, chili powder, garlic, thyme, ketchup, mayonnaise, and sea salt and black pepper, to taste, for the sauce.

Coat warm potatoes with sauce and garnish with microgreens, if using. Serve immediately.

Note: Store potatoes in a cool, dark place (our grandma uses a drawer in the kitchen). And never next to onions!

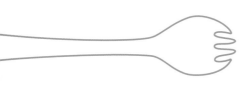

The Sporkie Scoop

FOR YOUR SMARTS Of the (at least) 50,000 varieties of pepper, the chili pepper is among the world's most popular spices. Only mammals are affected by the heat of capsaicin (the spicy-tasting stuff found in peppers). Birds are totally immune to it!

FOR YOUR PARTS What do potatoes and bandages have in common? A lot, it turns out. Boiled potato peels have been used directly on the skin in parts of the world as a treatment for burns, cuts, scrapes, etc. These dressings have antibacterial properties that can promote healing and prevent infection![20]

Creamed Onions with a Whole Wheat Bread Crumb Topping

Creamed onions are a holiday tradition we didn't know about until a few years ago, when a family member requested a veganized version of this dish. Having never had the dairy version, we did our homework. The result: a tearful but enjoyable experience, one that supposedly was better than the "real deal," according to our fam. If using fresh pearl onions, you may have a cleansing little cry, but it's well worth it! Unfortunately, once you make this a part of your holiday repertoire, it will stick, so be prepared to make this every year. **Serves 4-6**

Bread Crumb Ingredients

2 slices whole wheat bread, roughly chopped

2 teaspoons neutral tasting high-heat oil

½ teaspoon garlic powder

¼ teaspoon sea salt

½ teaspoon finely ground black pepper

½ teaspoon dried oregano

1 teaspoon agave nectar

1 teaspoon fresh lemon juice

Creamed Onion Ingredients

Water for boiling, salted

1 pound fresh pearl onions

3 tablespoons non-dairy butter

3 tablespoons spelt flour

1 cup soymilk creamer

½ teaspoon sea salt

¼ teaspoon finely ground black pepper

¼ teaspoon freshly grated nutmeg

1 teaspoon Champagne vinegar

1 teaspoon brown rice syrup

Directions

Preheat oven to 350°F.

For the bread crumbs: Place bread on a baking sheet. Drizzle with oil and sprinkle with garlic powder, sea salt, black pepper, oregano, agave and lemon juice. Toss to coat and bake for about 7-9 minutes or until crisp.

Pulse bread mixture in a food processor until bread crumb consistency is reached, and set aside.

For the creamed onions: Bring a large (6-quart) pot of salted water to a boil. Add pearl onions in their skin and cook, uncovered, for about 5 minutes. Drain onions and rinse with cold water to stop cooking.

(continued on next page)

Creamed Onions with a Whole Wheat Bread Crumb Topping

(continued from previous page)

Directions (continued)

To peel, slice both ends off and squeeze onion out of skin, discarding outer layers. Set onions aside.

In a medium (4-quart) pot, combine butter and flour. Whisk over medium heat, making a roux. Add creamer, sea salt, black pepper, nutmeg, vinegar and brown rice syrup. Whisking constantly, cook over medium heat for about 5 minutes, or until mixture is thick and creamy.

Grease an 8 x 8 baking dish and add onions. Coat with sauce mixture and top with bread crumb topping. Bake for about 25-30 minutes, or until mixture bubbles in the center.

Note: Though it may sound fun and easy to use frozen, pre-peeled pearl onions, they don't taste nearly as good in this recipe — so it's worth the cry!

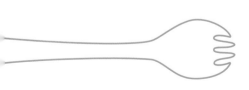

The Sporkie Scoop

FOR YOUR SMARTS Pearl onions are also called cocktail onions because they are used in boozy drinks! Generally pickled in a brine with turmeric and paprika, these darlings adorn your glass while adding a crisp sweetness to your Stoli Gibson (ideally: up, shaken, extra-dry).

FOR YOUR PARTS We avoid hydrogenated oils, partially hydrogenated oils and trans fats at all costs! They're made by heating veggie oil to over 400°F in the presence of certain metals and then forcing bubbling hydrogen through the crazy-hot oil for about 6 hours. Not only does this leach toxic metals into the oil, it distorts the molecules, causing too many health problems to list here.[21]

Green Bean Casserole with Spelt Bread Crumbs and Frizzled Shallots

Usually, when you make green bean casserole, everything is out of a can or a jar, but not in our kitch! We love the taste of fresh food, and using real veggies in this recipe really makes it shine (not to mention makes it healthier!). Also, it's usually served around the holidays, when you may want to show off your vegan cooking skills to friends and fam—so go to any dinner party confident, with this dish as your date. **Serves 4-6** (photo on p. 57)

Ingredients

3 tablespoons non-dairy butter

3 tablespoons unbleached all-purpose flour

1 cup crimini mushrooms, diced

2 cloves garlic, finely chopped

½ teaspoon sea salt

½ teaspoon finely ground black pepper

1 teaspoon evaporated cane sugar

1 tablespoon fresh lemon juice

2 cups unsweetened almond or soymilk

3 cups green beans, trimmed and cut into 1-inch pieces

2 tablespoons neutral tasting oil

2 shallots, finely sliced

Bread Crumb Ingredients

3 slices spelt bread, roughly chopped

1 tablespoon neutral tasting high-heat oil

¼ teaspoon sea salt

¼ teaspoon finely ground black pepper

¼ teaspoon garlic powder

½ teaspoon dried oregano

½ teaspoon paprika

1 teaspoon agave nectar

Directions

Preheat oven to 350°F.

Melt butter in a large (6-quart) pot over medium heat. Add flour, mushrooms and garlic, and stir until mushrooms are well coated in flour. Cook for about 2 minutes. Add sea salt, black pepper, sugar, lemon juice and almond or soymilk. Whisk over medium heat until sauce has thickened, about 5-7 minutes.

For the bread crumbs: While sauce is cooking, place bread on a baking sheet. Drizzle with oil and sprinkle with sea salt, black pepper, garlic powder, oregano, paprika and agave. Toss to coat, and bake for about 7-9 minutes, or until crisp.

(continued on next page)

Green Bean Casserole with Spelt Bread Crumbs and Frizzled Shallots

(continued from previous page)

Directions (continued)

Pulse mixture in a food processor until bread crumb consistency is reached. Set aside.

Grease a shallow casserole dish and add green beans. Add sauce mixture and stir to coat. Top with bread crumbs and bake for about 30 minutes, rotating once halfway through. Bake until top is golden and center is bubbling.

While casserole is cooking, heat a small (2-quart) pot, and add 2 tablespoons oil. Add sliced shallots and cook until crisp, about 1 minute.

Remove and drain on paper towels, and set aside.

When casserole is finished cooking, add frizzled shallots around rim of the casserole and serve warm.

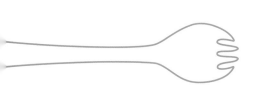

The Sporkie Scoop

FOR YOUR SMARTS   Cream of mushroom soup was traditionally used to make this dish, but not anymore! In that can, HALF of the calories come from fat!

FOR YOUR PARTS   The antioxidants found in green beans can help prevent cholesterol from sticking to blood vessels—preventing heart attacks and strokes![22]

Crispy Brown Rice Cakes with Adzuki Beans and Scallions

If you're in the mood to make a dish that is really satisfying and super simple, make these! The combination of adzuki beans and brown rice creates a complete protein. If you eat these as a snack, or as part of your meal, you will feel balanced and energized. This is one of Heather's favorite recipes, so when you make them in your kitchen, she'll be there—just let her know what time!

Yields about 10-12 (2-inch) cakes

Ingredients

2 cups water

1 cup short grain brown rice

3 tablespoons tamari (wheat-free)

2 tablespoons brown rice vinegar

2 tablespoons brown rice syrup

1 teaspoon hot pepper sesame oil

⅓ cup panko bread crumbs, plus 1 cup for coating patties

4-5 scallions finely chopped (about ⅓ cup)

1 (16-ounce) can adzuki beans, rinsed

2 tablespoons neutral tasting high-heat oil

Directions

Bring water to a boil in a large (6-quart) pot and add rice. Cover, reduce heat to a simmer, and cook about 35-40 minutes, or according to package.

Let rice cool slightly and place in a large bowl. Add tamari, brown rice vinegar, brown rice syrup, and sesame oil. Stir to incorporate all ingredients. Add ⅓ cup bread crumbs, ¼ cup scallions and adzuki beans. Stir mixture together well, mashing some adzuki beans into mixture with a wooden spoon, until mixture holds together.

Place remaining bread crumbs in a shallow dish and set aside.

Form rice mixture into 2-inch patties.

Heat a large sauté pan and add high-heat oil. Roll patties in bread crumbs and pat gently to remove excess crumbs.

Cook patties over medium heat for about 3-5 minutes, or until golden. Flip and cook for an additional 2-3 minutes.

Serve warm and garnish with remaining scallions.

Note: Panko are Japanese-style bread crumbs and they are a bit more coarse than standard bread crumbs. If you can't find them, use store-bought or homemade (see recipe on p. 52).

The Sporkie Scoop

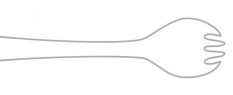

FOR YOUR SMARTS Thinking about soaking your own beans? If you've been intimidated, just stick with this plan: Cover them with about 3 inches of water in a bowl, soak them for 8-12 hours (or overnight), rinse them, and then cook in a fresh batch of water over low-medium heat for 1-2 hours. Cooking time varies from bean to bean!

FOR YOUR PARTS Brown rice fights colon cancer in more ways than one! It is a concentrated form of fiber AND has a trace mineral in it called selenium, which is known to substantially reduce the risk of colon cancer.[23]

Quinoa Salad with Fennel and White Beans in a Light Lemon Vinaigrette (gf)

Quinoa is good on its own, but with a few goodies it achieves greatness! This salad is so fresh and easy to prepare that it will become a regular in your cooking repertoire. Because it cooks in only 15 mins, you won't have any reason to microwave a meal ever again! **Serves 4-6**

Ingredients

2 cups water for boiling, salted

1 teaspoon extra-virgin olive oil

¾ cup white quinoa

¼ cup red quinoa

1 cup cooked cannellini beans, or 1 (15-ounce) can cannellini beans, rinsed

1 bulb fennel, finely chopped, plus stalks

1 tablespoon agave nectar

1 tablespoon mustard, stone ground or German

2 tablespoons fresh lemon juice, plus grated zest of 1 lemon

1 tablespoon extra-virgin olive oil

½ teaspoon sea salt, plus to taste

½ teaspoon finely ground black pepper, plus to taste

5-6 leaves fresh basil, finely chopped (plus extra leaves for garnish)

Directions

In a medium (4-quart) pot, combine salted water and olive oil, and bring to a boil.

Meanwhile, dry roast quinoa in a medium sauté pan (with no oil), stirring until fragrant, about 3 minutes. Add roasted quinoa to boiling water and cook for 12-14 minutes, or until all liquid is absorbed.

Transfer cooked quinoa into a large bowl and add beans, fennel, agave, mustard, lemon juice and zest, and olive oil. Toss together until well mixed. Season to taste with sea salt and black pepper. Top with basil. Serve warm or at room temperature.

Note: To create a more traditional salad, use baby lettuces or salad greens as a base, and top with the quinoa salad mixture.

The Sporkie Scoop

FOR YOUR SMARTS Quinoa, an amazing strength-building food, is technically a seed and not a grain — and it's quite political! It was cultivated by the Incas, but the Spanish conquistadors declared it illegal to grow (so illegal it was punishable by death). Eat up!

FOR YOUR PARTS Fennel is great for your digestion! It has aspartic acid, a strong carminative and anti-spasmotic. What does that mean in English? It helps remedy the toots.

Miso-Glazed Japanese Eggplant

If you happen to pass by some fresh Japanese eggplant at your local farmer's market, snag 'em and don't look back (after paying, of course). This recipe is the perfect way to use your eggplant because broiling gives it incredible texture, and it cooks up in 10 minutes or less! Serve these with some brown rice and a salad and you will be in *rakuen* ("heaven" in Japanese). **Serves 4-6**

Eggplant Ingredients

4-5 small Japanese eggplants

2 tablespoons neutral tasting high-heat oil

2 teaspoons fresh lemon juice

½ teaspoon sea salt

¼ teaspoon finely ground black pepper

Miso Glaze Ingredients

2 tablespoons light miso paste

1 tablespoon mirin (a sweet cooking sake)

2 tablespoons sake

2 teaspoons neutral tasting high-heat oil

1 teaspoon hot pepper sesame oil, or toasted sesame oil

1 tablespoon brown rice vinegar

2 tablespoons brown rice syrup

Directions

Preheat oven broiler to high.

Slice eggplant into long strips, about ¼-½ inch thick. Don't peel. Place eggplant on a large, rimmed baking sheet and coat with oil, lemon juice, sea salt and black pepper.

Broil eggplant on center rack for 4-5 minutes. Remove and flip. Broil for an additional 3-4 minutes. Remove from oven, leaving broiler on.

For the miso glaze: Whisk miso, mirin, sake, oil, sesame oil, vinegar and brown rice syrup in a medium bowl. Keep whisking until smooth.

Brush eggplant with miso glaze and broil for an additional 4 minutes. Stir and broil for an additional 4-5 minutes, until mixture is bubbling and eggplant looks golden brown.

Note: Some ovens only offer one broil setting or have the broiler in the lower portion of the oven, so check out your oven before creating this recipe. If you don't have a broiler, you can make this dish on a barbecue.

The Sporkie Scoop

FOR YOUR SMARTS Miso is a fermented paste made by combining cooked soybeans, beneficial mold (like koji), salt and various grains, such as rice or barley. This combination is fermented for 6 months to as long as many years. The three basic types are soybean miso (hatcho), barley miso (mugi) and rice miso (kome). The longer a miso has been aged, the stronger the flav.

FOR YOUR PARTS Eat eggplant — your brain will thank you! This veggie contains a phytonutrient called nasunin, which helps protect the lipid (fat) cells in our brains. Brain cell membranes are almost all lipids, so caring for them is super important.[24]

Grilled Asparagus with an Herb Pine Nut Sauce (gf)

This side dish is the perfect partner with so many main courses. It goes well with everything from Seitan Scallopini (see p. 119) to a veggie burger, so you will be inclined to make this often. Oh, and did we mention that this dish is packed with aphrodisiacs? So it can't hurt to make this on V-day to woo the one you love. **Serves 6-8**

Grilled Asparagus Ingredients

1 large bunch fresh asparagus, bottoms trimmed

2 tablespoons neutral tasting high-heat oil

½ teaspoon sea salt

½ teaspoon fresh lemon juice

Herb Pine Nut Sauce Ingredients

½ cup pine nuts

1 tablespoon neutral tasting oil

⅓ cup unsweetened almond or soymilk

½ teaspoon sea salt

¼ teaspoon finely ground black pepper

2 tablespoons fresh lemon juice, plus grated zest of 1 lemon

2 cloves roasted garlic (for roasting directions, see p. 2)

3 sprigs fresh thyme, stemmed and finely chopped

2 sprigs fresh oregano, stemmed and finely chopped

Directions

Heat a grill pan over medium heat and drizzle asparagus with oil. Place asparagus on grill and cook for about 3 minutes, or until grill marks appear. Flip and grill on other side. Sprinkle with sea salt and lemon juice and set aside.

For the sauce: Dry-roast pine nuts in a saucepan over low heat until lightly browned and fragrant. Remove and place in a high-powered blender or food processor. Add oil, almond or soymilk, sea salt, black pepper, lemon juice and zest, and roasted garlic. Blend until smooth. Fold in chopped herbs (reserving some for garnish). Set aside until ready to use.

When ready to serve, drizzle asparagus with pine nut sauce and sprinkle with additional fresh herbs.

The Sporkie Scoop

FOR YOUR SMARTS Why are asparagus a bit on the expensive side? Because each one is hand-harvested! So shell it out for this member of the lily family, and don't think twice.

FOR YOUR PARTS Pine nuts are a heart-strengthening food! They have tons of magnesium and potassium, a mineral combo that helps your heart beat strong! Store pine nuts in the fridge to make them last as long as you can.[25]

Mashed Potatoes with Caramelized Onions and Crispy Sage (gf)

We don't need heart-stopping cream and butter to make a rich dish of mashed potatoes—times have changed! The crispy sage adds a crunch, creating texture, and the caramelized onions add a sweet softness that rounds this dish out, making mashed potato perfection. **Serves 4-6**

Potato Ingredients

Water for boiling, salted

3-4 large organic russet potatoes, diced

2 tablespoons non-dairy butter, plus 2 tablespoons

3 cloves roasted garlic (for roasting directions, see p. 2)

1 brown onion, sliced into thin strips

2 teaspoons brown rice syrup

½ teaspoon sea salt, plus to taste

½ teaspoon freshly ground black pepper, plus to taste

½ teaspoon dried oregano

1 tablespoon fresh lemon juice, plus grated zest of 1 lemon

¼ cup unsweetened almond or soymilk, plus more as needed

Crispy Sage Ingredients

3 tablespoons neutral tasting high-heat oil

8-10 leaves fresh sage

Directions

Bring a large (6-quart) pot of salted water to a boil. Add potatoes and cook until tender, about 12-15 minutes.

While potatoes are cooking, add 2 tablespoons butter and roasted garlic to a large bowl and set aside.

Heat a sauté pan to medium heat and add remaining butter. Add onion and cook for about 2 minutes to soften. Add brown rice syrup, sea salt, black pepper and oregano, and cook on low heat for 5-7 minutes.

When potatoes are finished, drain and add them to large bowl containing butter and garlic. Mash potatoes with a potato masher and incorporate lemon juice and zest, almond or soymilk,

sea salt and black pepper into the potatoes. Season to taste with additional sea salt and black pepper.

For crispy sage: Heat a small sauté pan with oil over medium-high heat. Cook sage leaves until crisp, about 2-3 minutes.

To serve, top one scoop of potatoes with 1 tablespoon onions and a sprinkle of sage.

Note: For the crispy sage, make sure fresh leaves are very dry before using. Moisture will cause splattering in the sauté pan, so don't wash leaves right before frying.

The Sporkie Scoop

FOR YOUR SMARTS Brown rice syrup is a natural sweetener that is about half as sweet as sugar. It's made by steeping brown rice with enzymes, then straining off fermented liquid and cooking some more! It is a polysaccharide, which digests easily in the bod.

FOR YOUR PARTS Ever wonder why onions make you cry like a baby? They absorb sulfur from the soil, turning it into a personalized defense mechanism. Those sulfur compounds are a real tearjerker! But let it out, 'cause those tears dilute the acid and relieve the stinging sensation in your peepers.

"Fried" Green Tomatoes

Green tomatoes may be unripe, but they are not lacking in flavor. If you can find green heirloom tomatoes, even better! This dish is a Southern delicacy usually served with a spicy remoulade sauce. If you need a quick recipe to put one together — get a little of your favorite vegan mayo, some sweet pickle relish and a dash of hot sauce, stir and you're done! Don't even try this with ripe tomatoes, because they will become squishy, and the beauty of this dish is in the firmness of the tomatoes. **Yields 9-12 pieces**

Ingredients

4 large green tomatoes,
or green heirloom tomatoes

Dash sea salt, plus ¼ teaspoon,
plus ¼ teaspoon

Dash black pepper, plus ¼ teaspoon,
plus ¼ teaspoon

1 cup unbleached all-purpose flour

⅛ teaspoon cayenne pepper,
plus ⅛ teaspoon

1 cup yellow cornmeal

¼ teaspoon garlic powder

¼ cup neutral tasting high-heat oil

½ cup unsweetened almond
or soymilk, curdled with 1 teaspoon
unfiltered apple cider vinegar

Directions

Slice tomatoes into ½-inch-thick pieces, cutting off ends so rounds are flat. Season with dash of sea salt and black pepper; let rest about 5 minutes.

Place flour in a medium bowl and season with ¼ teaspoon each sea salt and black pepper and ⅛ teaspoon cayenne. Set aside.

Add cornmeal to a second medium bowl and add remaining sea salt, black pepper, cayenne and garlic powder. Whisk to incorporate, and set aside.

Preheat a large, stainless steel sauté pan (not aluminum or cast iron), and add oil.

Place curdled almond or soymilk in a bowl. Coat each tomato slice first in flour mixture, then dip tomato into curdled almond or soymilk mixture. Finally, coat tomato in cornmeal mixture until well covered. Repeat for all, then place in sauté pan.

Cook in batches of 4 or 5, without overcrowding pan. Cook for about 3 minutes over medium heat or until golden; flip and cook for an additional 2-3 minutes. Place cooked tomatoes on paper towel-lined plate. Serve warm.

Note: Always store tomatoes at room temp, because putting them in the fridge changes the flavor and texture, making them bitter and mealy.

The Sporkie Scoop

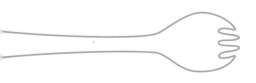

FOR YOUR SMARTS Traditionally, green tomatoes are soaked in an egg wash to make the crust stick — but we would never use an egg, not even one that is "cage-free"! Why? Because "cage-free" doesn't mean the chicken has a healthy life, with sunshine and a proper pecking order. Even cage-free eggs come from chickens that may have been de-beaked, fed numerous antibiotics and hormones — and the male chicks are killed because they can't produce eggs and are considered "useless" to the egg industry.

FOR YOUR PARTS Don't make these fried green tomatoes in an aluminum or cast iron pan, because the flavor will become metallic. The acid in the tomatoes can bind with the metals. It's time to bust out your stainless steel!

Green Apple and Cashew Sourdough Stuffing

Eating stuffing is one of our favorite parts of the holidays and Thanksgiving. This dish is pretty much a meal on its own, because we created it knowing that at Thanksgiving, when you are veg, sometimes you get stuck with the side dishes ... so if you bring one item to share, make it filling! The cashews add some protein to this dish, meaning you will feel filled up and energized instead of heavy and sleepy like those who ate the bird. Is it November yet? **Serves 6-8**

Ingredients

½ cup non-dairy butter
3 shallots, finely chopped
4-6 leaves fresh sage, finely chopped
2 green apples, medium dice
1 teaspoon sea salt
1 teaspoon finely ground black pepper
½ cup toasted cashews

1 loaf sourdough bread,
cut into large dice
1½ cups vegetable broth
(low-sodium)
2 tablespoons maple syrup
2 tablespoons unfiltered
apple cider vinegar

Directions

Preheat oven to 375°F.

In a medium (4-quart) pot, heat butter over medium heat. When hot, add shallots and cook until translucent, about 3-4 minutes. Add sage, apples, sea salt and black pepper, and continue to cook until apples are soft. Remove from heat and fold in cashews.

In a large bowl, add bread, vegetable broth, maple syrup and vinegar. Fold in apple mixture.

Pour stuffing mixture into a greased 8 x 8 baking dish and bake for about 30-40 minutes, or until bubbles appear in center of dish.

The Sporkie Scoop

FOR YOUR SMARTS Sourdough bread gets its sour quality because of the proportion of yeast to bacteria in the starter. The longer the starter has been around, the more flavorful the sourdough. A starter will keep for hundreds of years if cared for properly.

FOR YOUR PARTS Apples will be your tummy's saving grace this holiday. They are high in insoluble fiber, which can get the poop party started ... and if it's on overdrive, the pectin will help calm down the runs. Sorry, we know it's not appetizing, but it's a part of life.

Twice-Baked Potatoes with a Broccoli and Cheese Filling (gf)

This dish is the food of our childhood (we were never light eaters). Making these potatoes is a lot of fun, and they go over really well with the whole fam. Substitute some spinach for the broc, or add some black beans and corn for a little variation.
Serves 8-10

Ingredients

8-10 organic russet potatoes

Dash neutral tasting high-heat oil

Water for boiling, salted

2 crowns broccoli, roughly chopped

⅓ cup non-dairy butter

¾ cup vegan cheddar cheese, plus additional for topping (optional)

2 cloves garlic, finely chopped

1 tablespoon brown rice syrup

3 tablespoons fresh lemon juice

2 teaspoons dried basil or dill

1 teaspoon sea salt

½ teaspoon finely ground black pepper

Directions

Preheat oven to 375°F.

Place whole potatoes on a large baking sheet and coat with a small amount of oil. Bake for about 45-60 minutes, or until potatoes are soft.

Remove from oven and let potatoes cool. When cool, slice each potato in half lengthwise and place back on baking sheet. Keep oven on.

Bring a small (2-quart) pot half full of salted water to a boil, and cook broccoli for about 2 minutes or until bright green. Drain and set aside.

Using a melon baller or spoon, remove filling from each potato half and place in a large bowl, leaving potato skins intact. Set empty skins aside. Add butter to potato filling and mash with a potato masher until smooth. Add cheese, garlic, brown rice syrup, lemon juice, basil or dill, sea salt, black pepper and broccoli, and mix.

Place about ¼ cup of mixture into each potato half, and top with additional cheese if desired.

Bake potatoes for an additional 15 minutes, or until cheese is melted and tops are slightly browned.

Note: To make it easier on yourself, try roasting potatoes in advance, and scooping them out once they are cooled.

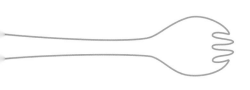

The Sporkie Scoop

FOR YOUR SMARTS Though Spanish conquistadors came to Peru in the 1500s in search of gold, they found something better—potatoes! Incas, who had been eating potatoes since around 500 B.C., didn't enjoy potatoes just because they were tasty; they worshiped them as healing tools for skin wounds and other medicinal uses.

FOR YOUR PARTS So why use a vegan cheddar cheese instead of dairy cheese? Dairy cheese contains casein, a cow's milk protein. And according to *The China Study,* diets that consist of over 20% of calories from milk protein result in cancer and tumor growth, among many other health problems. Plant-based protein-rich diets inhibit cancer growth or have the potential to reverse the growth of certain cancers.[26]

Broccolini in a Pecan Brown "Butter" Brandy Sauce (gf)

Broccolini isn't actually baby broccoli, so let's not treat it that way! This hybrid of Chinese cabbage and kale is all growed up. So get it drunk, get it buttery, and then get it in your mouth. **Serves 6-8**

Ingredients

Water for boiling

2 bunches broccolini, ends trimmed

3 tablespoons non-dairy butter

2-3 shallots, finely chopped

1 clove garlic, finely chopped

½ cup toasted pecans, coarsely chopped

2 tablespoons fresh lemon juice, plus grated zest of 1 lemon

¼ teaspoon sea salt, plus to taste

¼ teaspoon finely ground black pepper, plus to taste

1 tablespoon brown sugar

2 tablespoons brandy (optional)

Directions

Bring a medium (4-quart) pot of water to a boil. Add broccolini and cook 3-4 minutes, maintaining a steady boil. Drain in a colander, then transfer broccolini to a clean kitchen towel and pat dry.

In a large sauté pan over medium heat, melt butter. Add shallots, garlic and pecans. Sauté until shallots are soft and pecans are fragrant, about 3-5 minutes.

Add broccolini to pan and toss to coat mixture. Continue heating until broccolini has some blackened tips, about 3-5 minutes. Add lemon juice and zest, sea salt and black pepper.

Sprinkle broccolini tips with brown sugar and douse in brandy (if using). Cook for 2 more minutes, or until broccolini looks caramelized. Season to taste with sea salt and black pepper. Serve warm.

If preparing in advance: Before you are ready to eat, reheat in a warmed sauté pan and cook over medium heat for about 4-5 minutes, or until warmed through.

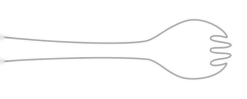

The Sporkie Scoop

FOR YOUR SMARTS Brandy, which is a spirit produced by distilling wine, can be served at room temp (a.k.a. neat) or on the rocks (with ice cubes). Our other fave drink with brandy is a veganized Brandy Alexander, using soy creamer instead of dairy cream.

FOR YOUR PARTS Broccolini is a cruciferous veg, a category that is thought to be a cancer preventive and fighter because of its high antioxidant and anti-inflammatory properties.[27]

Scallion Pancakes with a Sweet and Sour Dipping Sauce

If we don't make these scallion pancakes every few months, we seriously miss them. There is something about the texture and the way they are shaped that makes them so delish and fun to eat. This sweet and sour sauce is quite a good companion with these incredible pancakes — but, of course, use the sauce on whatever needs a little sweet and sour kick! **Yields 14-16 pancakes**

Pancake Ingredients

1¼ cups whole wheat pastry flour

1¼ cups unbleached all-purpose flour

1 teaspoon sea salt, plus to taste

½ teaspoon finely ground black pepper, plus to taste

1 cup water, salted

2 tablespoons roasted sesame oil

4 stems scallions, thinly sliced (about ¼ cup)

3-4 tablespoons neutral tasting high-heat oil, divided

Sweet and Sour Sauce Ingredients

¼ cup maple syrup

½ teaspoon sea salt

½ cup pineapple juice

2 tablespoons tomato paste

2 tablespoons brown rice vinegar

2 tablespoons tamari (wheat-free)

1 teaspoon grated fresh ginger

1 teaspoon toasted sesame oil

1 tablespoon arrowroot powder

2 tablespoons water

Directions

Add flours, sea salt and black pepper to a large bowl, and whisk.

Bring salted water to a boil and carefully pour into measuring cup. Fold hot water into flour mixture with a wooden spoon, until ball of dough is formed. Let rest for 30 minutes, covered with a damp cloth.

Place dough on a large, lightly floured board and roll into a large rectangle, about ¼-inch thick. Drizzle dough with sesame oil, and sprinkle with additional sea salt and black pepper. Evenly spread sliced scallions over dough.

Starting with longer side of dough that is facing you, roll it up from bottom to top, making a long coil. Slice coil into 8 pieces, each about 3 inches long.

Twist each piece 2-3 times and flatten into a pancake shape with your hand or a rolling pin. You will be able to see a spiral shape in the top surface of the pancake. Roll each pancake out to about a 4- or 5-inch round.

Heat a sauté pan over medium-high heat. Add 2 teaspoons oil per batch. Cook only 1 or 2 pancakes at a time and let sear for 1 minute. Cover with lid and cook pancake for 2 additional minutes on that same side. Remove lid and flip. Cook for an additional 2 minutes, or until well browned on both sides. Repeat process for remaining pancakes, adding 2 teaspoons oil to pan for each batch. Serve warm.

(continued on next page)

Directions (continued)

For the sauce: In a small (2-quart) pot over medium heat, combine maple syrup, sea salt, pineapple juice, tomato paste, vinegar, tamari, ginger, and sesame oil. Whisk constantly and cook for about 3 minutes, or until mixture begins to thicken.

In a small separate bowl, whisk together arrowroot powder and water. When sauce is fairly thick, add arrowroot mixture and cook for 1 more minute. Remove from heat and set aside.

Serve warm with pancakes

Note: This sauce will keep in the refrigerator for up to 2 weeks.

The Sporkie Scoop

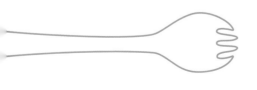

FOR YOUR SMARTS Ready to have your mind blown? A mature pineapple is actually made of up to 200 little fruits that come together to form a spiral around the central core! OMG! Pineapples are a symbol of hospitality, so bring one to a housewarming party and show your friends how much you care.

FOR YOUR PARTS A scallion (a.k.a. green onion or spring onion) is really an immature stem and bulb of an onion. But its healing properties are very adult. Scallions have anti-fungal and anti-microbial properties, and they're a great digestive aid. Not bad for a little onion relative.[28]

Southwest Black Bean and Corn Mini Burgers with a Smoky Paprika Cashew Cheese

There is something so appealing about eating mini foods, right? We love these petite burgs because they give you all the flavor of a large veggie burger, packed into a compact-sized snack. The gluten-free cashew cheese is crucial for making these burgers truly special—and feel free to go wild on the fixin's. **Yields 12 mini burgers** (photo on p. 81)

Ingredients

1 tablespoon neutral tasting high-heat oil, plus 2 tablespoons

½ large onion, finely diced

2 cloves garlic, finely diced

½ cup corn, fresh or frozen

½ large red or orange bell pepper, finely chopped

Dash sea salt, plus ½ teaspoon

¼ teaspoon finely ground black pepper

1 (15-ounce) can black beans, rinsed

¼ teaspoon chipotle powder

1 tablespoon vegan Worcestershire sauce

1 tablespoon fresh lemon juice

2 teaspoons agave nectar

¾ cup rolled oats

1 cup bread crumbs or 2 slices spelt bread (see recipe for homemade bread crumbs on p. 52)

Cashew Cheese Ingredients (gf)

¾ cup cashews

½ teaspoon garlic powder

½ teaspoon sea salt

2 teaspoons agave nectar

½ teaspoon smoked paprika

2 tablespoons neutral tasting oil

¼ cup unsweetened almond or soymilk

1-2 tablespoons fresh lemon juice

3 sprigs fresh thyme, stemmed and finely chopped

Whole grain mini burger buns

Ketchup, mustard, pickle relish, tomato and lettuce (optional)

Directions

Preheat large (6-quart) pot over medium heat and add 1 tablespoon oil. Add onion and garlic and cook for about 2 minutes. Add corn, bell pepper, dash of sea salt and black pepper. Cook until mixture is slightly browned, about 3-4 minutes, and set aside.

In a food processor, combine black beans, chipotle powder, ½ teaspoon sea salt, Worcestershire sauce, lemon juice and agave. Pulse together 5-8 times. Add oats and bread crumbs or spelt bread. Pulse until uniform, scraping down sides to further incorporate into food processor. Transfer to a large bowl.

(continued on next page)

Southwest Black Bean and Corn Mini Burgers with a Smoky Paprika Cashew Cheese

(continued from previous page)

Directions (continued)

Add cooked onion and pepper mixture to bowl and fold into veggie burger mixture.

Heat a large sauté pan over medium heat and add remaining oil. With damp hands, form burgers into patties and place in heated pan. Cook for about 5 minutes on each side or until browned.

For the cashew cheese: In a large food processor or high-powered blender, pulse cashews, garlic powder, sea salt, agave, paprika, oil, almond or soymilk and lemon juice. Blend until smooth and uniform, scraping down sides of machine as needed. Fold in thyme once mixture is creamy.

Serve on a toasted mini bun with all of the fixin's!

Note: If you can't find mini burger buns, use dinner rolls—or serve patties topped with cashew cheese over baby greens, with the creamy basil dressing from the Southwest Chopped Salad (recipe on p. 39).

The Sporkie Scoop

FOR YOUR SMARTS   Voting hasn't always required paper and ink dots! People have used pebbles, marbles and loud cheering to cast their votes. But in ancient Greece and Rome, beans were used, a black bean meaning "no" and a white bean meaning "yes"!

FOR YOUR PARTS   Oats are a super nutrient-dense cereal grain that can actually help reduce cravings for cigarettes![29]

MAIN DISHES

MAIN DISHES

*(gf) indicates the recipe is gluten-free!

DIY: Homemade Tofu (and Homemade Soymilk) (gf)

The flavor of your own fresh tofu is unlike anything you can purchase in a store! And with this recipe, of course, you are learning how to make tofu, but you get a bonus recipe for homemade soymilk (since it's the first step to making tofu)! If you don't have an official tofu press, you can use anything you have around the house to shape your tofu — all you need is a way to drain it and you're set! If you fall in love with this process, you can go online to order a tofu-making kit, which usually comes with some coagulant. **Advance preparation required. Yields 1 block of tofu**

Ingredients

2 cups dry organic soybeans, soaked in water overnight

3 cups water, plus 3 cups, plus 7½ cups

1 tablespoon terra alba or 1 tablespoon nigari (natural coagulants), dissolved in 1 cup warm water

Directions

For the soymilk: Strain soaked soybeans in a colander and rinse. Add 1 cup soybeans to a blender with about 3 cups water, and blend into a smooth puree. Place in a large (6-quart) pot. Repeat blending process for remaining soybeans and additional 3 cups water. Place second portion in pot.

Add remaining 7½ cups water to pot of soymilk puree. Bring to a boil and then turn down and simmer, uncovered, for 7-10 minutes.

Over a large bowl, place a large cheesecloth or fine mesh bag on top of a strainer. Pour cooked mixture slowly into cloth, and then pull cloth together and twist, allowing milk to drip into bowl for a few minutes. With tongs (or a towel over your hand), squeeze out as much milk as possible.

The mixture is hot, so be careful. The solid mixture left in the cheesecloth is called okara. Don't throw it away before you see "For Your Smarts," next page.

For the tofu: Pour strained soymilk through a fine sieve into a large (6-quart) pot. Stirring frequently, heat soymilk to 180°F (do not boil), and remove from heat.

Pour dissolved coagulant mixture (terra alba or nigari) into hot soymilk and slightly agitate, but don't stir. Milk will begin to curdle. Allow to curdle for at least 3-5 minutes, undisturbed.

For soft tofu, curdling should be minimal; to make hard tofu, add more dissolved terra alba or nigari, or allow mixture to sit longer without being stirred.

To press the tofu: Put tofu mold in sink, or a larger baking dish, to allow liquid to drain off. Cover inside of mold with a cheesecloth that is much bigger than mold shape, with about 3 inches excess cloth draped over rim. Pour curdled soybean milk into mold, then fold over extra cheesecloth.

Place pressing board on top of cheesecloth. Put a weight on top to add pressure, making sure weight is evenly dispersed.

For soft tofu, 5 minutes of pressing is enough; for firmer tofu, press for 20 minutes or more. When tofu has been pressed, lift wrapped tofu from mold and uncover. Tofu can be stored in water in refrigerator for up to 1 week, or can be used right away.

Note: As far as economics go, making your own tofu is a bit pricier than the store-bought variety, but the wonderful taste makes it worth it!

The Sporkie Scoop

FOR YOUR SMARTS The pulp remaining in the cheesecloth when making tofu is okara. It is high in protein and fiber and can be made into veggie burgers or used in many dishes.

FOR YOUR PARTS Calcium sulfate and magnesium chloride are usually used to coagulate tofu, but those are the processed coagulants. The natural forms are terra alba (gypsum), which is used for softer or smoother tofu, and nigari, which is derived from sea water, for firmer tofu. When you don't have time to make your own tofu, look for nigari or gypsum on your packaged tofu label (instead of the synthetic versions), because they will be more natural.

DIY: Homemade "Chicken-Style" Seitan

Seitan (a.k.a. wheat meat, wheat gluten, mock meat, or just good ol' gluten) is the protein in wheat. Making your own seitan is a fun process, and it is very easy to do. Truly making it from scratch (with just wheat and water) it would take many hours, but you can purchase vital wheat gluten in the market or online nowadays, making the whole process much easier! And the added bonus of making your own seitan—besides being more delish—is that it is more economical too!

Yields about 4-5 cups seitan pieces

Seitan Ingredients

1½ cups vital wheat gluten flour

½ teaspoon garlic powder

½ teaspoon paprika

½ teaspoon sea salt

¼ teaspoon finely ground black pepper

¼ teaspoon turmeric

½ teaspoon dried oregano

2 tablespoons unfiltered apple cider vinegar

½ cup vegetable broth (low-sodium)

1 cup water

1 tablespoon vegan Worcestershire sauce

Simmering Broth Ingredients

6 cups vegetable broth (low-sodium)

3-4 cups water

1 tablespoon vegan Worcestershire sauce

2 bay leaves

Directions

For the seitan: In the bowl of a standing mixer with a dough hook, or a large bowl with a wooden spoon, mix together flour, garlic powder, paprika, sea salt, black pepper, turmeric and oregano. Add apple cider vinegar, vegetable broth, water and Worcestershire sauce, mixing until a mass forms.

Continue to knead seitan dough with dough hook for about 3 minutes, until a spongy, elastic dough is formed —or by hand for about 5-8 minutes, until it is difficult to pull apart. Slice seitan dough into large rounds, chunks or small pieces.

For the broth: Add vegetable broth, water, Worcestershire sauce and bay leaves to a large (6-quart) pot, and bring to a simmer.

Carefully place dough pieces in simmering broth. It is important that broth is not boiling when adding seitan pieces, to help with texture and consistency. Gently simmer dough pieces for 1 hour to 1 hour 15 minutes, stirring occasionally.

Remove from heat and let seitan cool in broth for at least 30 minutes.

Note: For an Asian-flavored broth, use tamari, grated ginger and rice vinegar for flavor! To store seitan, cook completely and keep in broth for up to 2 weeks in the refrigerator. To freeze seitan, completely drain, and store in plastic bags for months.

The Sporkie Scoop

FOR YOUR SMARTS Seitan, pronounced SAY-tan, is a very meat-like vegetarian protein simply made from the gluten of wheat. It has a long history in Japan, China and Korea, and wasn't popularized in the United States until the macrobiotic movement in the '60s.

FOR YOUR PARTS Seitan is an amazing alternative to animal protein. Here's why you should ditch the meat and embrace the wheat: A diet based on the consumption of animal protein (slightly less than 1 ounce per day) has been linked to many health problems, one of them being the formation of kidney stones! No thanks.[30]

Mushroom Bourguignon

When the weather is cold, and you are going to be home for a little while, this is the perfect dinner — and we mean perfect! It doesn't take long to get your ingredients in the pot, it just takes a while to cook this dish through. But the results are well worth it! You'll fill the house with the most delish scents west of the Seine. **Serves 4-6**

Ingredients

2 tablespoons extra-virgin olive oil

3-4 carrots, diced

1 large yellow onion, diced

1 cup pearl onions, peeled

2 cups crimini mushrooms, halved

1 cup button mushrooms, halved

1 cup toasted walnuts

1 organic russet potato, diced

1 cup frozen peas

4 cloves roasted garlic (for roasting directions, see p. 2)

3 cups dry vegan red wine (Pinot Noir preferred)

½ cup vegetable broth (low-sodium)

2 tablespoons tomato paste

6 sprigs fresh thyme, finely chopped

½ teaspoon sea salt, plus to taste

½ teaspoon finely ground black pepper, plus to taste

2 tablespoons non-dairy butter (room temperature)

3 tablespoons unbleached all-purpose flour

2 tablespoons brown rice syrup

French baguettes (organic preferred)

Directions

Heat olive oil in large, heavy (6-quart) pot over medium heat. Add carrots, yellow onion and pearl onions, and cook for about 3 minutes to start browning. Add mushrooms and walnuts, and cook for about 3 more minutes.

Add potato, peas and garlic, and stir. Add wine, vegetable broth, tomato paste, thyme, sea salt and black pepper. Bring to a simmer, then cover pot with a tight-fitting lid and cook over low heat for about 35-45 minutes, stirring occasionally.

While vegetable mixture is cooking, whisk together room temperature butter and flour in a small bowl.

Set aside.

After about 30 minutes of cooking, add brown rice syrup, and butter and flour mixture to pot, and stir.

Season to taste with sea salt and black pepper. Cook for an additional 5-10 minutes over low heat. Serve warm with a French baguette.

Note: The longer you cook this dish, the more flavorful it becomes, so put the heat on low and let this cook for up to 1 hour if you have the time, adding more wine as you go.

The Sporkie Scoop

FOR YOUR SMARTS Beef bourguignon used to be French "peasant" food because cooking the beef in wine for a long time made the cheaper and poorer quality meat tender and easier to eat. What a bummer. Today we veganize, modernize and create a dish we are all proud of.

FOR YOUR PARTS We all know that we can get omega-3 fatty acids from walnuts, right? If not, let's just pretend we did. Just ¼ cup of these bad boys has 90% of what we need for the day!

Seitan Wellington with a Creamy Spinach Sauce

This has become our Thanksgiving go-to dish! Though we love experimenting in the kitchen and coming up with new, creative recipes, we think Thanksgiving is a time to bust out your tried and true standbys. After all, you're probably facing some skeptics, and you don't want anyone to think that all vegans eat for T-givs is side dishes! Of course, this dish is elegant and can be served any time of year, so whenever you feel like creating something special, give this recipe a shot.

Yields 2 small or 1 large Wellington. Serves 6-8

Mushroom Filling Ingredients

1 tablespoon non-dairy butter

1 tablespoon extra-virgin olive oil

4 cups crimini mushrooms, finely chopped

2 large shallots, finely chopped

3 cloves garlic, finely chopped

3 sprigs fresh thyme, stemmed and finely chopped

2 tablespoons vegan red wine (Merlot or Cabernet Sauvignon)

¼ teaspoon sea salt

¼ teaspoon finely ground black pepper

2 tablespoons unbleached all-purpose flour

Seitan Filling Ingredients

2 packages "chicken-style" seitan, or 3 cups homemade seitan (see recipe on p. 86)

4 sprigs fresh thyme, stemmed and finely chopped

2 tablespoons mustard, stone ground or German

2 tablespoons vegan red wine (Merlot or Cabernet Sauvignon)

1 tablespoon maple syrup

¾ cup unbleached all-purpose flour, plus ¼ cup flour for rolling

Grated zest of ½ lemon

½ teaspoon smoked paprika

½ teaspoon sea salt

¼ teaspoon finely ground black pepper

1 package frozen puff pastry sheets, thawed

Creamy Spinach Sauce Ingredients

3 cups baby spinach, packed

1 tablespoon extra-virgin olive oil

1 clove garlic, finely chopped

1 teaspoon fresh lemon juice

¼ teaspoon sea salt

¼ teaspoon finely ground black pepper

¼ cup, plus 1 tablespoon soymilk creamer

Directions

Preheat oven to 400°F.

For the mushroom filling: In a large sauté pan, heat butter and olive oil. Add mushrooms, shallots and garlic. Cook over medium heat for about 2 minutes. Add thyme, wine, sea salt, black pepper and flour, and cook

(continued on next page)

Seitan Wellington with a Creamy Spinach Sauce

(continued from previous page)

Directions (continued)

for an additional 3-5 minutes, or until all the liquid has evaporated. Set aside to cool.

For the seitan filling: In a large food processor, combine seitan, thyme, mustard, wine, maple syrup, flour, lemon zest, paprika, sea salt and black pepper. Pulse until uniform, about 20 times, and set aside.

On a lightly floured surface, roll puff pastry out to about ⅛-inch thickness. To make one large Wellington, overlap 2 sheets by about 1 inch and press them

together at seam. Place mushroom filling in center of pastry and spread out, leaving about a 1- to 2-inch border on all sides. Top mushrooms with seitan filling and fold over puff pastry border to form a log shape, completely sealing filling.

If making two small Wellingtons, divide seitan and mushroom filling in half before forming each log shape, and proceed as directed above.

To bake, place one large, or two small Wellingtons, seam side down

on a greased baking sheet with rims. Make a couple of slits in top of pastry with a small knife. Bake for 40-45 minutes, until pastry is golden brown. Let cool for 10 minutes before slicing.

For the spinach sauce: Sauté spinach in a large sauté pan over low heat with olive oil, garlic, lemon juice, sea salt and black pepper, until wilted. In a blender, combine with soymilk creamer, and purée until smooth.

Serve sliced Wellington warm with spinach sauce.

The Sporkie Scoop

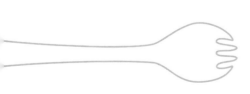

FOR YOUR SMARTS Arthur Wellesley, the Duke of Wellington, who helped defeat Napoleon, is credited with the name of this dish. He probably never set foot in the kitch to create this masterpiece — and we can almost guarantee he had never heard the word seitan — but we adore this recipe ... so thank you, Duke!

FOR YOUR PARTS The crimini mushrooms make this dish so much healthier than the beefy version! Criminis are made of a lot of water and are low in calories, but taste amazing, yay! They are also high in potassium, which is great for regulating blood pressure.[31]

Potato Gnocchi with Basil in a Roasted Shallot Cream Sauce

Don't be intimidated by a little piece of pasta. Making your own gnocchi isn't as difficult as your Italian grandma would like you to think it is. This recipe is a cinch, and you don't have to be Italian to master the perfect gnocchi. The sauce on this pasta is rich and full-bodied because of the roasted shallots. Feel free to improvise with a little red sauce, or if you feel like lightening it up, use our pesto recipe (p. 110) instead of the cream sauce. **Serves 4-6** (photo on p. 93)

Roasted Shallot Cream Sauce Ingredients

2 large shallots, peeled and thinly sliced

2 tablespoons neutral tasting oil, plus 1 tablespoon

Dash sea salt, plus ½ teaspoon

Dash finely ground black pepper, plus ½ teaspoon

1½ cups toasted cashews

⅔ cup water

½ cup unsweetened almond or soymilk

2 tablespoons fresh lemon juice

1 tablespoon red wine vinegar

1 tablespoon brown rice syrup

2 teaspoons dried herbs (oregano or thyme)

Gnocchi Ingredients

Water for boiling, generously salted

2 pounds small organic yellow or red potatoes, skins on, quartered

10-12 leaves fresh basil, finely chopped

Grated zest of 1 lemon

1 teaspoon sea salt

½ teaspoon finely ground black pepper

2 cups unbleached all-purpose flour, plus ½ cup for kneading

Extra-virgin olive oil, for drizzling

5-6 fresh basil leaves, finely chopped, for garnish

Directions

Preheat oven to 375°F.

For the sauce: In a small baking dish, combine sliced shallots, 2 tablespoons oil, dash sea salt and black pepper, and roast for 10 minutes. Remove from heat.

Add cooked shallots to a blender or food processor. Add cashews, water, almond or soymilk, remaining oil, lemon juice, vinegar, brown rice syrup, dried herbs, and ½ teaspoon each of sea salt and black pepper. Blend until creamy and uniform.

For the gnocchi: Bring a large (6-quart) pot of salted water to a boil. Add potatoes and cook for about 15 minutes, or until soft. Drain and transfer potatoes to a large bowl and cool for about 10 minutes. Mash potatoes with a potato masher or ricer. Add basil, lemon zest, sea salt and black pepper. Slowly incorporate flour with your hands and knead gnocchi dough until smooth and uniform, about 5-7 minutes.

(continued on next page)

Potato Gnocchi with Basil in a Roasted Shallot Cream Sauce

(continued from previous page)

Directions (continued)

Bring an additional large pot of water to a boil over high heat and add sea salt.

Meanwhile, to roll the gnocchi:
Divide dough into 4 segments and roll each segment into a long, 1-inch-thick coil. Cut coil into ¾-inch pieces (small pillows) and indent each piece of dough between your thumb and the tines of a fork, producing a ribbed look. Repeat for all pieces and set aside on a floured board until ready to boil.

With water at a boil, add gnocchi one at a time with a slotted spoon, cooking no more than 10-15 at once.

Gnocchi will sink, and after about a minute and a half will float to the top, indicating they are finished cooking. Remove from water and place in a large sauté pan. Coat with a drizzle of olive oil to prevent sticking.

Place large sauté pan containing cooked gnocchi over low heat, and cook for about 3 minutes, then add shallot cream sauce. Cook until heated through. Garnish with fresh basil and serve immediately.

The Sporkie Scoop

FOR YOUR SMARTS Potatoes have been cultivated for over 7,000 years, originally by the ancient Incas, and are native to the Andes mountains of Bolivia and Peru.

FOR YOUR PARTS Almond milk is one of our fave non-dairy milks. One cup of unsweetened almond milk is 40 cals, and it has 30% of your RDA of calcium and 25% of your RDA of Vitey D — and it tastes good, so how can you top that?[32]

Vietnamese Crêpe with a Mushroom-Bean Sprout Filling and a Spicy Tamari Dipping Sauce

Get crazy experimental with this crêpe recipe! Throw in any fresh veggies you have, and if you want some "oohs" and "aahs" from your dinner guests, make a giant one and serve it up right in front of them! **Yields 4-6 round eight-inch crêpes**

Crêpe Ingredients

½ cup regular coconut milk

2 tablespoons garbanzo bean (chickpea) flour

1 cup organic rice flour

½ cup arrowroot powder

1 teaspoon turmeric, plus more if desired

½ teaspoon sea salt

1½-2 cups water

Filling Ingredients

2 tablespoons, plus 2 teaspoons neutral tasting high-heat oil

2 scallions, thinly sliced (about 2 tablespoons)

1 onion, thinly sliced

1 package enoki mushrooms

12-15 crimini mushrooms, roughly chopped

2 cups organic mung bean sprouts

1 bunch red leaf lettuce, washed

1 small bunch mint leaves

Dipping Sauce Ingredients

1 clove garlic, coarsely chopped

1 red jalapeño pepper, seeds removed

¼ cup evaporated cane sugar or palm sugar

¼ cup brown rice vinegar

¼ cup tamari (wheat-free)

1 tablespoon ume plum vinegar

½ cup water

Directions

For the batter: Add coconut milk to a medium bowl and whisk in flours, arrowroot, turmeric, sea salt and water. Whisk until uniform.

Let batter rest for 30 minutes to overnight. Refrigerate if leaving overnight.

To make one crêpe: Heat 2 teaspoons oil in a large non-stick sauté or crêpe pan over medium-high heat. Add 1 teaspoon chopped scallion, 6 slices onion, ¼ package of enoki mushrooms, and 2-3 crimini mushrooms and cook for about 1 minute.

Ladle about ⅓ cup of crêpe batter into pan. Tilt and swirl pan to coat bottom and even out batter over ingredients. Cook for about 2-3 minutes over high heat or until edges look browned.

Add ½ cup bean sprouts to half of crêpe. Cover pan and cook over high heat for about 2 minutes. Fold crêpe in half. Remove from heat and carefully slide crêpe onto a serving plate. Repeat for remaining batter.

For the dipping sauce: Add garlic, jalapeño, sugar, rice vinegar, tamari, plum vinegar and water to a blender and blend until uniform. For a milder sauce, do not put jalapeño in blender; instead, slice it and add after sauce is blended.

Serve with lettuce leaves, mint and dipping sauce.

The Sporkie Scoop

FOR YOUR SMARTS Wild enoki mushrooms are darker in color because they see the light of the sun! Cultivated enokis are never exposed to light, so they are white.

FOR YOUR PARTS Even after they are harvested, bean sprouts maintain all of their nutritional properties until they are eaten!

Cashew Cream Fettuccine Alfredo with Sautéed Spinach and Cheese Crisps (gf)

The traditional version of this dish is known for its creamy, rich texture and its impact on your hips. Our Alfredo gives you the same fulfilled feelings without the side effects! Adding the cheese crisps makes this a delight to eat, because you get the crunch along with the creamy texture of the noodles. We like to toss in some greens whenever we get the chance, so throw in spinach, kale or chard for a boost of nutrients. **Serves 4-6**

Ingredients

6-8 cups water for boiling, salted

1 package (14-ounce) brown rice fettuccine

1 teaspoon neutral tasting oil

3 tablespoons non-dairy butter

2 large shallots, finely chopped

3 cups baby spinach, tightly packed

Alfredo Sauce Ingredients

1½ cups unsweetened almond or soymilk

1 cup soymilk creamer

2 cups cashews

¾ teaspoon sea salt

½ teaspoon finely ground black pepper

1 tablespoon light miso paste (non-barley)

2 tablespoons fresh lemon juice

¼ teaspoon freshly grated nutmeg

½ teaspoon dry mustard

3 tablespoons arrowroot powder, plus 2 tablespoons water, whisked to form a slurry

1½ cups shredded vegan cheese (Daiya brand)

Directions

Bring salted water to a boil in a large (6-quart) pot. Add fettuccine and cook as described on package, about 7-9 minutes. Drain and run under cold water. Place back in cooking pot with oil to prevent sticking. Toss to coat.

Heat a small (2-quart) pot and melt butter. Add shallots and cook over medium heat until soft, about 3 minutes. Remove shallots from pot, using a slotted spoon. Set aside in a small bowl.

Add spinach to same buttered pot and cook over medium heat until wilted, about 2 minutes. Remove from heat. Add spinach to cooked fettuccine.

For the Alfredo sauce: In a large blender or food processor, add almond or soymilk, creamer, cashews, sea salt, black pepper, miso, lemon juice, nutmeg, dry mustard and cooked shallots. Blend until smooth, about 3 minutes. Transfer to a large (6-quart) pot and heat for about 3-5 minutes, or until warm. Add arrowroot slurry, whisking until sauce thickens slightly, about 30-60 seconds.

For the cheese crisps: Preheat oven to 375°F. Sprinkle cheese on a baking sheet and bake for about 12-14 minutes, or until crisp. Let cool completely and break into large, uneven pieces to garnish the pasta.

To serve, add sauce to fettuccine and spinach and toss to coat. Serve warm with one piece of cheese crisp per serving.

The Sporkie Scoop

FOR YOUR SMARTS Fettuccine Alfredo was invented less than 100 years ago in Rome by a restaurateur named Alfredo di Lelio.

FOR YOUR PARTS The cashew (a seed, not a nut!) has a lower fat content than most nuts and contains monounsaturated fats, which are known to protect against heart disease.[33]

Personal Seitan Pot Pies with an Herb Biscuit Topping

Pot pie has been the ultimate comfort food for generations, so make this recipe when you are in need of some foodie TLC. Rather than getting a frozen version of this dish that has no love, a gross amount of sodium and tons of cals, use this recipe — with natural, whole ingredients — and you're guaranteed comfort without the guilties. **Serves 6**

Seitan and Vegetable Filling Ingredients

¼ cup non-dairy butter

¼ cup unbleached all-purpose flour

1 medium onion, finely chopped

1 large orange bell pepper, finely chopped

3 cloves garlic, finely chopped

1 tablespoon neutral tasting high-heat oil

2 cups seitan, cut into large dice (see homemade seitan recipe on p. 86)

½ cup fresh or frozen English peas

1 medium carrot, diced

1½ cups vegetable broth (low-sodium)

1 teaspoon dried oregano

1 teaspoon dried basil

2 tablespoons fresh lemon juice

¾ teaspoon sea salt

½ teaspoon finely ground black pepper

Biscuit Topping Ingredients

1¾ cups unbleached all-purpose flour

2 teaspoons non-aluminum baking powder

½ teaspoon baking soda

½ teaspoon dried oregano

½ teaspoon sea salt

¼ teaspoon finely ground black pepper

3 tablespoons non-dairy butter

¾ cup unsweetened almond or soymilk, curdled with 1 teaspoon unfiltered apple cider vinegar

2 teaspoons agave nectar

Directions

Preheat oven to 400°F.

For the filling: In a large (6-quart) pot over medium heat, whisk to combine butter and flour, creating a roux. Add onion, bell pepper and garlic, and cook for about 3 minutes.

In a sauté pan, add oil and seitan. Sauté until browned, about 3-5 minutes, and set aside.

In the pot with the roux, add peas, carrot, vegetable broth, oregano, basil, lemon juice, sea salt and black pepper. Stir continuously over medium heat until mixture thickens, about 5-7 minutes. Add seitan and cook for an additional 2 minutes. Remove from heat.

(continued on next page)

Directions (continued)

For the biscuit topping: In a large bowl combine flour, baking powder, baking soda, oregano, sea salt and black pepper, and whisk until uniform. Cut butter into flour with pastry whisk until mixture resembles a coarse meal. Add curdled almond or soymilk and agave to the flour mixture and knead just until mixture holds together.

To assemble: Place ¼ cup seitan and vegetable filling in a ramekin or cocotte. Top each with about 3 tablespoons biscuit topping. Biscuit mixture will be sticky, so use damp hands to put topping on the ramekin. Place filled ramekins on a rimmed baking sheet and bake until crust is golden brown and filling is bubbling, about 30 minutes.

Note: This recipe makes 6 individual servings. If you have an 8-inch round soufflé pan, you can create one large pot pie that will serve 6 people instead.

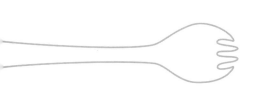

The Sporkie Scoop

FOR YOUR SMARTS   Remember fifth-grade biology? You might recollect hearing about Gregor Mendel, an Austrian monk and scientist who used green peas and their plants to understand heredity, inheritance of traits and genetics. It's amazing how much one can learn from a veggie!

FOR YOUR PARTS   Dudes—cook this dish for your lady during her time of the month. Why? Because there are carrots up in here and they can help relieve PMS and crampies! And trust us, she won't want to cook.[34]

Tempeh Sausages with a Mushroom Gravy

These sausages are deceptively easy to make! They may look and taste as if you were hard at work in the kitch all day, but they are actually ready in only 20 minutes — and we're talkin' with the gravy! These are also super appropriate to make for Thanksgiving dinner or holiday parties because they use hearty herbs like sage and make your house smell amazing! **Yields 10-12 large sausages** (photo on p. 103)

Sausage Ingredients

3 (8-ounce) packages soy tempeh

2 tablespoons extra-virgin olive oil

¼ cup fresh lemon juice

2 tablespoons balsamic vinegar

2 tablespoons mustard, stone ground or German

1 tablespoon brown rice syrup

1 teaspoon sea salt

½ teaspoon finely ground black pepper

½ teaspoon red pepper flakes

4 leaves fresh sage, finely chopped

8 fresh chives, finely chopped

1 teaspoon fennel seeds

⅓ cup organic bread crumbs or cornmeal (see recipe for homemade bread crumbs on p. 52)

⅓ cup neutral tasting high-heat oil

Coating Ingredients

1 cup organic bread crumbs or cornmeal (see recipe for homemade bread crumbs on p. 52)

½ teaspoon sea salt

½ teaspoon finely ground black pepper

½ teaspoon dried sage

Gravy Ingredients

2 tablespoons non-dairy butter

2 tablespoons unbleached all-purpose flour

2 cups crimini mushrooms, roughly chopped

2 cups vegetable broth (low-sodium)

8-10 leaves fresh sage, finely chopped

1 teaspoon fresh lemon juice

2 teaspoons brown rice syrup

½ teaspoon sea salt

½ teaspoon finely ground black pepper

Fresh herbs for garnish, optional

Directions

Fill a large (6-quart) pot with about 1 inch of water and place steamer basket in pot. Bring to a simmer with lid on. Slice tempeh into large pieces. Place in steamer basket, cover and steam for about 5-7 minutes. This removes any bitter flavor tempeh may have.

In a food processor, add steamed tempeh, olive oil, lemon juice, vinegar, mustard, brown rice syrup, sea salt, black pepper, red pepper flakes, sage, chives, fennel seeds and ⅓ cup bread crumbs or cornmeal. Pulse until mixture is uniform, about 30 pulses.

(continued on next page)

Directions (continued)

For the coating: Place 1 cup bread crumbs or cornmeal, sea salt, black pepper and dried sage in a large shallow bowl. Whisk together and set aside.

To form the sausages: Using hands, scoop about 2 tablespoons of sausage mixture and form into large, elliptical shapes. Encrust each tempeh sausage in coating mixture.

Preheat a large sauté pan and add high-heat oil. Place sausages in pan. Cook over medium heat for about 3 minutes on each side, until well browned.

For the gravy: Heat a medium (4-quart) pot over medium heat. Add butter and flour. Whisk until a paste forms. Add mushrooms and coat in flour mixture. Cook for about 2 minutes. Add vegetable broth and whisk until uniform. Add fresh sage, lemon juice, brown rice syrup, sea salt and black pepper. Cook for about 5-7 minutes or until mixture has thickened.

To serve, top sausages with warm gravy and garnish with fresh herbs.

The Sporkie Scoop

FOR YOUR SMARTS Historically, gravy is this: thickened meat juices, flour and fat — all whisked together and served in a gravy boat. Grody to the max. Our gravy breaks from tradition by not harming a soul and still providing the thick, rich texture we are all looking for.

FOR YOUR PARTS Eating sage during the holidays is a great idea because of its anti-microbial properties. It's also a powerful decongestant and can help fight a cold, flu or fever![35]

Frosted Tempeh Loaf

This dish will throw your taste buds back to the '50s and make you feel like Betty Crocker is looking over your shoulder, watching your every move. Make this pretty loaf when you are in need of some comfort and old-fashioned home cookin'.
Serves 4-6

Tempeh Loaf Ingredients

1 tablespoon neutral tasting high-heat oil

1 medium onion, finely chopped

2 carrots, grated

1 garnet red beet, scrubbed, peeled and quartered

2 (8-ounce) packages soy tempeh, crumbled

1 slice spelt bread or whole grain bread

¼ cup vegan Worcestershire sauce

1 tablespoon fresh lemon juice

1 tablespoon brown rice syrup

½ teaspoon sea salt

½ teaspoon finely ground black pepper

1 tablespoon mustard, stone ground or German

¼ cup ketchup, plus ¼ cup

1 tablespoon fresh herbs (sage or thyme), finely chopped

Mashed Potato Layer Ingredients

Water for boiling, salted

2 large organic russet potatoes, diced

1 tablespoon non-dairy butter

2 teaspoons lemon juice

¼ cup unsweetened almond or soymilk

½ teaspoon sea salt

½ teaspoon finely ground black pepper

Directions

Preheat oven to 350°F.

Heat oil in a large sauté pan over medium heat. Add onion and cook for about 5 minutes or until soft. Set aside.

In a food processor, pulse carrots and beet. Add tempeh, cooked onion, bread, Worcestershire sauce, lemon juice, brown rice syrup, sea salt, black pepper, mustard and ¼ cup ketchup. Pulse until uniform. Add fresh herbs and stir until uniform.

Lightly coat a 9 x 5 loaf pan with oil. Press tempeh loaf mixture firmly into prepared loaf pan.

Bake for 35-40 minutes or until loaf pulls away from sides of pan and looks slightly dry.

While loaf is baking, bring a large (6-quart) pot of salted water to a boil. Add potatoes and cook until tender, about 12-15 minutes.

(continued on next page)

Frosted Tempeh Loaf

(continued from previous page)

Directions (continued)

When loaf is finished, let stand for 10 minutes to cool, then invert onto a serving platter. While warm, rub all sides of loaf with remaining ketchup.

When potatoes have finished cooking, drain and add to a large bowl. Mash potatoes with butter, lemon juice, almond or soymilk, sea salt and black pepper.

With a spatula, spread mashed potatoes evenly over entire surface of tempeh loaf.

Turn oven to broil (high setting preferred). Broil frosted tempeh loaf until well browned, about 2-3 minutes.

Note: If you don't have a broiler, cook frosted tempeh loaf at 375°F for about 5-7 minutes.

The Sporkie Scoop

FOR YOUR SMARTS Worcestershire sauce was originally created in India, but it got its name because it was first bottled in Worcester, England. This sauce is not only amazing in our loaf, but it rocks a ranch dressing, Bloody Mary or any veggie burger.

FOR YOUR PARTS Garnet red beets are a high-fiber veggie whose color indicates that they're great for your blood. They can help your circulation, fight anemia and ease constipation (just sayin').[36]

Roasted Butternut Squash and Sage Lasagna with a Creamy Béchamel Sauce

When you are in the mood to make a satisfying lasagna that will feed your whole family, use this recipe. You can even get a little arm workout by putting this into, and taking it out of, the oven. Lasagna isn't supposed to be light and fluffy! The flavors of the slightly sweet butternut squash and creamy béchamel sauce really come together with the addition of the strong flavor of sage. We like using spelt lasagna noodles for this, because even though it is a nice, filling recipe, we always try sneaking in a few more nutrients. **Serves 4-6** (photo on p. 109)

Lasagna Ingredients

1 large butternut squash (or skip roasting step and use 2 (15-ounce) cans pureed butternut squash)

6-8 cups water, salted

1 box spelt lasagna noodles

2 tablespoons non-dairy butter
6-8 leaves fresh sage, finely chopped
2 teaspoons fresh lemon juice
1 teaspoon agave nectar
¼ teaspoon sea salt
Finely ground black pepper, to taste

2 teaspoons extra-virgin olive oil
3 cups baby spinach, tightly packed

Béchamel Sauce Ingredients

⅓ cup non-dairy butter

⅓ cup unbleached all-purpose flour

4 cups unsweetened almond or soymilk

1 teaspoon dry mustard powder

1 teaspoon garlic powder

½ teaspoon sea salt

½ teaspoon finely ground black pepper

1 bay leaf

Dash freshly grated nutmeg

3 tablespoons fresh lemon juice

Directions

Preheat oven to 375°F.

To roast the butternut squash:
Turn squash on its side. Slice in half, separating round base from longer top of squash. If squash is large, cut longer piece in half again. Place cut sides down on an greased baking sheet. Roast squash for 40-60 minutes, depending on size. Test for doneness by inserting a knife. When no resistance is given, it is finished. Remove seeds and stringy fiber. Scoop out 3 cups of cooked butternut squash and set aside in a large bowl.

Bring salted water to a boil in a large (6-quart) pot. Add noodles and cook as described on package, about 7-9 minutes. Drain.

(continued on next page)

Roasted Butternut Squash and Sage Lasagna with a Creamy Béchamel Sauce

(continued from previous page)

Directions (continued)

In the large bowl containing cooked squash, use a potato masher to combine butter, sage, lemon juice, agave, sea salt and black pepper.

In a medium sauté pan, cook olive oil and spinach over medium heat until wilted, about 2 minutes. Remove from heat.

For the béchamel sauce: Heat a medium (4-quart) pot over medium heat and add butter. Whisk in flour and create a paste, making a roux. Add almond or soymilk, mustard powder, garlic powder, sea salt,

black pepper, bay leaf, nutmeg and lemon juice. Whisk, stirring continuously. Cook for about 7 minutes, or until béchamel sauce looks thick and creamy. Discard bay leaf.

To assemble: First, spread a layer of béchamel on the bottom of a lasagna dish. No need to spray dish with cooking oil. Next, add a layer of lasagna noodles, making sure to cover entire bottom of dish.

Add a layer of butternut squash mixture, then another layer of noodles. Top with béchamel sauce.

Add a spinach layer and then another layer of noodles, and top with béchamel. Repeat sequence until all filling is used. Finish dish with a layer of lasagna noodles covered in a thick layer of béchamel sauce.

Bake for about 35 minutes, or until bubbles appear in center of lasagna.

The Sporkie Scoop

FOR YOUR SMARTS   Fresh herbs are generally added to dishes just before serving them, while dried herbs are used earlier in the cooking process. The scent and flavor diminish in dried herbs over time, so adding them to your ingredients helps the flavors pop!

FOR YOUR PARTS   Botox is the fashionable anti-aging solution, but butternut squash has been the naturally occurring solution for thousands of years. It is super-high in carotenoid viteys and has anti-aging orange pigments that protect cells from damage caused by free radicals![37]

Creamy Pistachio Pesto over Brown Rice (gf)

Although we love pine nuts, sometimes we vary up the flavors of this classic Italian dish by using pistachios. The pistachio flavor is very rich, the roasted garlic is very creamy, and the miso paste gives our pesto the salty, cheesy texture we all want. Use this flavorful pesto sauce on pizza, over brown rice or quinoa pasta, or on a sandwich as a spread! **Yields 1 cup pesto sauce. Serves 6**

Ingredients

4 cups water, for boiling

2 cups short grain brown rice

6-8 cloves roasted garlic (for roasting directions, see p. 2), or 3 cloves raw garlic

⅓ cup, plus 2 tablespoons extra-virgin olive oil

3 tablespoons fresh lemon juice

½ cup pistachio nuts, shelled, plus 2 tablespoons for garnish

2½ cups fresh basil leaves, packed, plus for garnish

1 tablespoon light miso paste (non-barley)

½ teaspoon sea salt, plus to taste

½ teaspoon finely ground black pepper, plus to taste

1 cup cherry tomatoes, sliced in half lengthwise

½ cup pitted Kalamata olives, sliced into thirds

Directions

Preheat oven to 375°F.

Bring water to a boil in a medium (4-quart) pot, add brown rice, cover and cook according to package directions, about 35 minutes. Set aside.

For the pesto sauce: While rice is cooking, place garlic, oil and lemon juice in a food processor and blend for 15 seconds. Add pistachios, basil, miso, sea salt and black pepper, and blend for about 30 seconds, or until smooth.

Toss brown rice with pesto sauce, until all rice is coated evenly. Add tomatoes and olives. Season to taste with sea salt and black pepper. Garnish with a sprig of fresh basil and remaining pistachios. Serve warm.

The Sporkie Scoop

FOR YOUR SMARTS Pesto comes from the Italian term for pounded or crushed, so give this sauce an old-school touch and make it with a mortar and pestle — getting your workout before you eat! Hand-crushing also helps to bring out the flavor of the basil.

FOR YOUR PARTS We love garlic, we really do. But we love it even more when it's roasted because you don't get that breath. The reason it makes you stink is because garlic's essential oils actually permeate your lung tissue! Chewing gum and brushing won't work, but roasting really helps.

Cornmeal and Herb-Crusted Tofu Feta Croquettes (gf)

Quick and delicious is the name of the game with these croquettes. When you are over veggie burgers, but still want something high in protein as your main course—these are your new BFF. The texture of these croquettes is crunchy on the outside, making them the perfect main course for any light Mediterranean meal. Pair them with our Niçoise salad (p. 40) for the ultimate pleasing combo. **Yields about 15 small croquettes**

Ingredients

1 (14-ounce) block extra-firm tofu, pressed and drained (see recipe for homemade tofu on p. 84)

1 teaspoon fresh oregano, finely chopped

2 teaspoons fresh thyme, finely chopped

1 tablespoon brown rice syrup

2 tablespoons fresh lemon juice, plus grated zest of 1 lemon

2 teaspoons neutral tasting high-heat oil

¼ teaspoon sea salt

¼ teaspoon finely ground black pepper

1 tablespoon light miso paste (non-barley)

1 heaping tablespoon vegan cream cheese

2 teaspoons red wine vinegar

Ingredients (continued)

½ cup yellow cornmeal, plus 1½ cups

½ teaspoon dried oregano

½ teaspoon dried basil

2 tablespoons neutral tasting high-heat oil

Directions

In a large bowl, crumble tofu with your hands. Add oregano, thyme, brown rice syrup, lemon juice and zest, oil, sea salt, black pepper, miso, cream cheese, vinegar and ½ cup cornmeal. Stir until well mixed.

In a separate shallow dish, add remaining 1½ cup cornmeal, oregano, basil, sea salt and black pepper. Mix until uniform.

Using hands, form tofu-feta mixture into small patties and coat each patty in cornmeal mixture. Pat off any excess cornmeal.

Heat a large sauté pan and add 2 tablespoons high-heat oil. Add croquettes and over medium heat, cook on each side for about 3-4 minutes, or until browned and crisp.

The Sporkie Scoop

FOR YOUR SMARTS Have you ever wondered why there's a bit of lime or lime ash in your corn tortillas? It's because when people subsisted mostly on corn, which is low in niacin, an epidemic of pellagra (an often fatal disease!) broke out. Native Americans discovered that cooking with lime kept them from getting sick. That's because the lime increased their niacin absorption rate!

FOR YOUR PARTS Oregano, a member of the mint fam, contains anti-microbial agents (thymol and carvacrol) that can naturally fight infections and have also been shown to inhibit the growth of certain types of bacteria![38]

South Carolina Barbecue Tofu Sandwich

Many regions of the United States have their own spin on barbecue sauce and each has its special ingredients. This South Carolina-style sauce we created has the blend of sweet, spicy and sticky that we adore about good ol' BBQ. And just because we're slathering this sauce on tofu doesn't mean it wouldn't be great on tempeh, seitan, portobello mushrooms — or any other veggies you can put on a grill. **Serves 6-8**

Barbecue Sauce Ingredients

1 tablespoon neutral tasting high-heat oil, plus 2 tablespoons

½ medium onion, finely chopped

2 cloves fresh garlic

1½ small cans (about ¾ cup) tomato paste

½ cup unfiltered apple cider vinegar

½ cup evaporated brown sugar

¼ cup brown rice syrup

¼ cup maple syrup

2 tablespoons vegan Worcestershire sauce

1 teaspoon sea salt, plus dash

½ teaspoon finely ground black pepper, plus dash

½ teaspoon ground allspice

¼ teaspoon celery seed

1 tablespoon dry mustard powder

¼ teaspoon cayenne pepper, plus to taste

½ cup water

1 (14-ounce) block extra-firm tofu (see recipe for homemade tofu on p. 84)

4-6 whole grain burger buns or dinner rolls

Directions

To make barbecue sauce, put a large (6-quart) pot over medium heat and add 1 tablespoon oil, onion and garlic, and cook until soft, about 3 minutes.

Add tomato paste, vinegar, brown sugar, brown rice syrup, maple syrup, Worcestershire sauce, sea salt, black pepper, allspice, celery seed, mustard powder and cayenne. Add water. Cook for 5-10 minutes over medium heat, stirring occasionally. The longer the sauce is cooked, the better the flavor.

Preheat a large sauté pan or grill pan and add remaining oil. Cut tofu into ¼-inch slices. Place tofu in pan and sprinkle with a dash of sea salt and black pepper. Cook for about 4 minutes on first side until well browned. Flip and coat tofu with barbecue sauce. Cook for an additional 5-7 minutes, flipping tofu over gently, until it looks well coated and is heated through.

Serve warm on a toasted whole grain bun or roll with all of the fixin's!

The Sporkie Scoop

FOR YOUR SMARTS There's a diff between BBQing and grilling. Here's the deal: Barbecuing means that the heat is low and foods are slow cooked, whereas grilling is done directly over a flame and food is cooked at a higher heat more quickly.

FOR YOUR PARTS Apple cider vinegar is really just freshly pressed apple juice, fermented at room temp!

Barbecue-Style Spelt Pizza with Caramelized Onions and Tempeh Bacon

Ordering a pizza is pretty easy, and nowadays some places even let you order online—but forget all of that, because making your own pizza is so satisfying ... and it's not hard to do! This pizza is flavorful, and once you make pizza from scratch, you won't look at delivery the same way. Of course this recipe can be adapted in many ways! Use a traditional pizza sauce and vegan cheese for a slight twist, or top this pie with any veggies you can get your hands on.

Advance preparation required. Serves 6-8

Pizza Dough Ingredients

½ cup warm water, plus ½ cup at room temperature

1 package (¼-ounce) active dry yeast, or 2¼ teaspoons dry yeast

2 cups spelt flour

1 cup unbleached all-purpose flour, plus more as needed, for kneading

1 teaspoon evaporated cane sugar

1 teaspoon dried basil

1 teaspoon sea salt

½ teaspoon finely ground black pepper

2 tablespoons extra-virgin olive oil

2 teaspoons neutral tasting high-heat oil

Barbecue Topping Ingredients

2 tablespoons non-dairy butter

2 medium onions, cut into thin slices (about 2 cups)

¼ teaspoon sea salt

¼ teaspoon finely ground black pepper

2 teaspoons evaporated cane sugar

1 teaspoon fresh lemon juice

1 tablespoon fresh thyme, finely chopped

½ cup yellow cornmeal

2 cups South Carolina barbecue sauce (see recipe on p. 114)

1 package tempeh bacon, cut into 1-inch pieces

Neutral tasting high-heat oil, for brushing crust

8-10 leaves fresh basil, finely chopped

Directions

For the dough: In a small bowl, combine ½ cup warm water and yeast. Whisk gently and let sit for about 7-10 minutes, or until yeast blooms.

In a mixing bowl or electric mixer bowl, combine spelt flour and 1 cup all-purpose flour, sugar, basil, sea salt and black pepper. Whisk to combine.

Add yeast mixture, olive oil, and remaining ½ cup water to flour mixture. Knead for 8-10 minutes, or until dough is smooth and very elastic. If using an electric mixer, set up dough hook. If kneading by hand, additional flour may be required.

(continued on next page)

(continued from previous page)

Directions (continued)

Transfer to a large bowl and coat dough in high-heat oil. Cover with damp towel and let dough double in size, about 1-2 hours.

Preheat oven to 425°F. If using a pizza stone, preheat stone in oven.

For the caramelized onions: Preheat a large sauté pan over medium heat. Add butter and onions and sauté until soft, about 5-7 minutes. Add sea salt, black pepper, sugar and lemon juice. Add thyme and cook for an additional 2 minutes.

To assemble the pizza: Sprinkle a flat baking sheet or pizza peel (paddle) with cornmeal, and shape dough into a 13-inch round over cornmeal, making sure there are no spots where the dough sticks. Spread South Carolina barbecue sauce evenly over flattened pizza dough. Top with caramelized onions and tempeh bacon. Brush rim of crust with oil. If using pizza stone, carefully transfer from peel into oven.

Bake for about 15-18 minutes, or until crust looks brown and slightly dry. Top with fresh basil.

The Sporkie Scoop

FOR YOUR SMARTS Word on the street is that the Italian pizza we all know and love evolved from an early Egyptian flatbread. It wasn't until after WWII that American GIs in Italy encountered these lovely pies and made them into an American classic — and a staple of every college kid's diet.

FOR YOUR PARTS Tomato paste can help prevent some serious health probs, including atherosclerosis — a condition where fats build up in your arteries and can block them, leading to heart attack or stroke.[39]

Seitan Scallopini with Sautéed Mushrooms in a Red Wine Sauce

This main course is one of our more boozy dishes. The red wine adds a lot of flavor to the sauce, and we love the way the sautéed mushrooms and red wine complement each other. Though this dish may appear difficult or fancy-pants, it's quick to put together and goes with a wide array of side dishes. **Serves 4-6** (photo on p. 121)

Ingredients

2 packages (2 cups) "chicken-style" seitan, or 2 cups homemade seitan (see recipe on p. 86)

2 tablespoons balsamic vinegar

1 tablespoon neutral tasting oil

2 tablespoons maple syrup

1 tablespoon fresh lemon juice

½ teaspoon sea salt, plus 1 teaspoon

½ teaspoon finely ground black pepper, plus ½ teaspoon

1½ cups spelt flour or unbleached all-purpose flour

1 teaspoon garlic powder

1 teaspoon dried basil

½ teaspoon dried thyme

¼ cup neutral tasting oil

Red Wine Mushroom Sauce Ingredients

2 tablespoons non-dairy butter

2 cups crimini mushrooms, roughly chopped

2 teaspoons unbleached all-purpose flour

¾-1 cup vegan red wine

1 tablespoon maple syrup

1 tablespoon fresh lemon juice, plus grated zest of ½ lemon

½ teaspoon sea salt

½ teaspoon finely ground black pepper

Fresh herbs for garnish

Directions

Slice seitan into long, thin strips. Depending on style of seitan used, pieces will vary in size. Place seitan in a large bowl and add vinegar, oil, maple syrup, lemon juice, and ½ teaspoon each of sea salt and black pepper. Toss to coat seitan evenly.

In a separate shallow dish, whisk together flour, garlic powder, basil, thyme, 1 teaspoon sea salt and ½ teaspoon black pepper. Coat each piece of seitan in seasoned flour mixture.

Heat a large sauté pan and add remaining ¼ cup oil. Cook each coated piece of seitan over medium heat for about 3 minutes on each side, allowing them to brown and crisp.

(continued on next page)

Seitan Scallopini with Sautéed Mushrooms in a Red Wine Sauce

(continued from previous page)

Directions (continued)

Once seitan is cooked, remove from pan and place on a large plate lined with paper towels.

For the sauce: In same pan, after seitan pieces are removed, add butter and mushrooms, and sauté over medium heat for about 2 minutes. Add flour and cook for an additional 2 minutes. Add wine, maple syrup, lemon juice and zest, sea salt and black pepper. Continue cooking for 2 more minutes, whisking constantly, until sauce is slightly thickened.

Place cooked seitan on a platter and drizzle with mushroom sauce. Serve warm and garnish with fresh herbs.

The Sporkie Scoop

FOR YOUR SMARTS   Scallopini is a term that refers to a thin, breaded cutlet, and in our case, they're made of seitan. For a little variation, try using tempeh in this dish or substitute a crisp, vegan white wine instead of red.

FOR YOUR PARTS   The maple syrup in this recipe, used to add a touch of sweetness, is a really powerful ingredient. It has lots of manganese and zinc, which boosts your immune system! And we're talking about pure maple syrup, not high-fructose corn syrup and caramel color in disguise.

Creamy Baked Macaroni and Cheese with a Spelt Bread Crumb Topping

This mac 'n' cheese is one of our most popular dishes! It goes over well with everyone, not only vegans, and has even converted a few non-vegans on the spot. For a really cute presentation, bake it in individual, brightly colored ramekins, and give each of your guests their own scoop of heaven. **Serves 4-6**

Ingredients

6-8 cups water for boiling, salted

12 ounces quinoa or spelt elbow macaroni

Sauce Ingredients

⅓ cup non-dairy butter

⅓ cup unbleached all-purpose flour

2½ cups unsweetened almond or soymilk

⅔ cup nutritional yeast flakes

½ teaspoon sea salt

½ teaspoon finely ground black pepper

2 cloves garlic, finely chopped

1 tablespoon light miso paste

¼ cup fresh lemon juice

2 teaspoons mustard, stone ground or German

½ cup homemade bread crumbs (see recipe on p. 52)

Directions

Preheat oven to 350°F.

Bring salted water to a boil in a large (6-quart) pot. Add macaroni and cook as described on package, about 7-9 minutes.

For the sauce: Heat a medium (4-quart) pot over medium heat. Add butter and flour. Whisk together to form a paste, creating a roux. Add almond or soymilk, nutritional yeast, sea salt, black pepper, garlic, miso, lemon juice and mustard. Cook for about 7 minutes, stirring constantly, until sauce is thick and creamy.

Once macaroni is finished cooking, drain and add to pot with sauce. Mix thoroughly to coat. Place mixture in a greased 8 x 8 baking dish, or 6 personal ramekins or cocottes, and top with homemade bread crumbs.

Bake for about 30-35 minutes, or until bubbles appear in center of dish. Serve warm from the oven.

The Sporkie Scoop

FOR YOUR SMARTS The word macaroni comes from the Italian phrase "Ma caroni", meaning "How very dear!"—because this style of pasta is so petite, it makes everyone happy.

FOR YOUR PARTS Just embrace nutritional yeast. And when you purchase it (to get your B-12 and tons of other vities), be sure to buy high grades, sometimes called "primary," which are usually grown on sugar beets or molasses. And don't call us, crying, when your pee is neon yellow—it's normal!

Ginger, Maple and Mustard-Glazed Tempeh (gf)

This insanely delish main dish recipe is one of our sneakiest! No one will know that this actually takes less than 15 minutes to prepare, so keep a package of tempeh on hand at all times for quick and easy protein. If you happen to have some leftovers (and you probably won't), throw them over a salad and you'll be satisfied and energized for hours! **Serves 4-6**

Ingredients

2 (8-ounce) packages soy tempeh

1 piece fresh ginger (about 2 inches), peeled

2 cloves garlic, finely chopped

¼ cup extra-virgin olive oil

¼ cup fresh lemon juice

2 tablespoons mustard, stone ground or German

3 tablespoons maple syrup

1 teaspoon sea salt

½ teaspoon red pepper flakes

Directions

Fill a large (6-quart) pot with about 1 inch of water and place a steamer basket inside. Bring to a simmer with lid on. Slice tempeh into 6-8 half-inch strips. Place in steamer basket, cover, and steam for about 5 minutes. This removes any bitter flavor the tempeh may have.

While tempeh is steaming, grate ginger over a large bowl with a fine grater. Add garlic, olive oil, lemon juice, mustard, maple syrup, sea salt and red pepper flakes. Whisk until uniform. Add steamed tempeh to mixture, coating each piece.

Heat a large sauté pan over medium heat and pour tempeh and sauce mixture into pan. No need for additional cooking oil. Cook for about 4 minutes on each side until well browned, flipping occasionally, until sauce has been absorbed.

Serve warm.

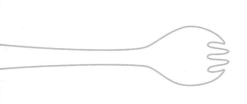

The Sporkie Scoop

FOR YOUR SMARTS Tempeh originated in Indonesia, where it is still sold today in marketplaces, wrapped in banana leaf. (Who needs plastic?!)

FOR YOUR PARTS Ginger is redic! It has anti-inflammatory compounds called gingerols that have been used to reduce pain associated with arthritis and other inflammatory issues![40]

DESSERTS

DESSERTS

*(gf) indicates the recipe is gluten-free!

Apple and Pear Tarte Tatin

Created by sisters who ran a hotel in France, the Tarte Tatin was made by accident one night when a tired sister burned her caramelized apples in an attempt to make an apple pie. She rescued her dish by throwing her pastry base on top of the apples and shoving it in the oven! This shows you that even a flub can become a masterpiece! **Serves 6**

Ingredients

¾ cup evaporated cane sugar, plus 2 teaspoons

3 tablespoons water

2 tablespoons maple syrup

2 large Pink Lady or Gala apples

2-3 Bosc pears

1-2 teaspoons fresh lemon juice, plus grated zest of 1 lemon

Dash vanilla extract

3 tablespoons unbleached all-purpose flour, plus 1 tablespoon

2 tablespoons non-dairy butter

⅛ teaspoon sea salt

¼ teaspoon ground cinnamon

1 sheet frozen puff pastry, thawed

Directions

Preheat oven to 400°F.

Over medium heat in a 10-inch cast-iron sauté pan, combine ¾ cup sugar and water, and heat. Reduce heat to medium-low. Add maple syrup and cook mixture until it turns a rich, golden caramel color, stirring often, about 6-7 minutes.

Cut apples and pears into large, even slices and place in a large bowl. Add lemon juice and zest, remaining sugar and vanilla extract, and toss to coat. Add 3 tablespoons flour and toss to coat.

Add butter and remaining flour, sea salt and cinnamon to sauté pan with caramel mixture. Whisk well and remove from heat. Arrange coated apple and pear pieces in sauté pan, rounded sides down, fitting as many into pan as possible. Place sheet of puff pastry on top of apples and pears. Tuck any excess edges under and be sure to press pastry onto top. Make two small slits in pastry to allow steam to escape. Place in oven and bake for 10 minutes. Reduce heat to 375°F and bake until pastry is golden brown, about 25 minutes.

Remove from oven and let cool, about 10 minutes. Loosen edges with a knife. Carefully place a large plate (face-down) over sauté pan and flip to invert. Serve warm or at room temperature.

Note: There will be some liquid in the Tarte Tatin, so flip it over the sink.

The Sporkie Scoop

FOR YOUR SMARTS The Tarte Tatin is interpretive and has been made using all sorts of ingredients, such as pineapple, peaches, bananas — and even tomatoes!

FOR YOUR PARTS The most exciting nutritional benefit of pears is their high fiber content. Eat one of these and you are already getting 25% of your suggested daily intake!

Apple Pie Milkshake

Apple pie is an American classic. We adore it, especially when served à la mode. This little treat is like that whole scenario, only blended. It's so fun to eat one of these shakes, and the best part is that you don't have to take the time to make a whole apple pie! It's worth buying malt shop glasses, a jukebox and a T-bird just to get the full effect of sipping this amazing dessert in a diner during the Fifties. **Serves 4-6**

Apple Pie Ingredients

1 Fuji apple, sliced into thin strips

1 Granny Smith apple, sliced into thin strips

1 teaspoon ground cinnamon

¼ teaspoon ground cloves

¼ teaspoon freshly grated nutmeg

3 tablespoons maple syrup

1-2 teaspoons fresh lemon juice

⅛ teaspoon sea salt

2 teaspoons arrowroot powder

2 sheets frozen puff pastry, thawed

Shake Ingredients

1 quart non-dairy vanilla ice cream

2 cups unsweetened almond or soymilk

2 teaspoons cinnamon sugar (optional for topping)

Apple slices for garnish (optional)

Directions

Preheat oven to 400°F.

For the pie: In a medium bowl, combine apple slices, cinnamon, cloves, nutmeg, maple syrup, lemon juice, sea salt and arrowroot powder, and mix filling together until uniform. Set aside.

Lay sheets of puff pastry on a baking sheet lined with parchment paper or silicone baking mat (or use cooking spray), and divide filling evenly between sheets. Place filling on half of each sheet and fold other half over, making 2 separate pies. Tuck in sides so no filling bubbles out during baking. Make 2 small slices on top of each pie to allow steam to escape.

Bake for about 15 minutes or until golden brown and bubbling in center. Allow to cool completely.

Place cooled apple pies on a cutting board and dice into small pieces.

For the shake: Add ice cream and almond or soymilk to a blender and blend until smooth. For a thicker shake, add more ice cream; for a thinner consistency, add more almond or soymilk.

To serve, fold in pieces of cooled apple pie and pour into tall glasses. Top with cinnamon sugar and a slice of apple for the rim of the glass (optional). Serve with a spoon or thick straw.

The Sporkie Scoop

FOR YOUR SMARTS   Clove, a dried, unopened pink flower bud, is nature's original breath mint. Used in China over 2,000 years ago, people put cloves in their mouths while talking to the Emperor so as not to offend him!

FOR YOUR PARTS   Apples have been used to reduce fevers because of their cooling and moistening nature![41]

Grandma's Bird's Nest Cookies Rolled in Pistachios

Twelve years ago, when we told Grandma Jeanette that we'd gone vegan, she got to work! She veganized each and every recipe that she'd created (she was the baker and Grandpa Manny was the cook). Grams currently lives in L.A., spending 7 days a week with her identical twin sister, and continues to amaze us during our weekly dinners with her baked treats. **Yields 16-20 cookies**

Cookie Ingredients

1 cup pistachios
½ cup non-dairy butter
½ cup unrefined cane sugar
1 tablespoon vanilla extract
½ teaspoon almond extract
2 cups unbleached all-purpose flour
2 teaspoons egg replacer, dry
½ teaspoon ground cinnamon
¼ teaspoon sea salt
3-4 tablespoons unsweetened almond or soymilk

"Egg Wash" Ingredients

½ cup, plus 1 tablespoon unsweetened almond or soymilk
1 teaspoon egg replacer, dry

½ cup jam (raspberry or strawberry), or orange marmalade

Directions

Preheat oven to 350°F.

Place pistachio kernels on a baking sheet and roast for about 5-7 minutes, or until fragrant. Pulse pistachios in a food processor until fine, about 5-8 times. Place roasted ground pistachios in a shallow dish and set aside.

In the bowl of a standing mixer, cream butter and sugar. Add vanilla and almond extracts. Whisk until uniform and creamy.

Add the flour, egg replacer, cinnamon and sea salt. Add 3-4 tablespoons almond or soymilk. Whisk until a ball of dough forms, but don't overwhisk because this makes dough gummy and chewy.

For the "egg wash": In a separate bowl, combine unsweetened almond or soymilk and egg replacer. Set aside. This creates an "egg wash" to make nuts stick to the outside of the cookies.

Form dough into small balls and roll each ball in egg wash, and then in ground nuts. Set on a greased cookie sheet.

Make a thumb indentation on top of each cookie and fill with about ½ teaspoon jam or marmalade. Place on a greased baking sheet.

Bake for about 25-27 minutes, until jam is bubbling and cookies look golden brown.

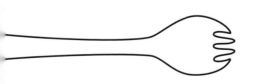

The Sporkie Scoop

FOR YOUR SMARTS What's the diff between jam and jelly, anyways? Jam uses real fruit, while jelly uses fruit juice — they are both mixed with sugar and sometimes pectin.

FOR YOUR PARTS Though it's not conventional in a cookbook to talk about pooping, read on ... pistachios will deal with your poop probs by easing constipation![42]

Chocolate Peanut Butter Mousse with a Crunchy Topping (gf optional)

This dessert is so decadent, no one will believe it's vegan. And not only that ... no one will be able to guess that there is tofu in this little sucka. We're not usually the kind of vegans that slide tofu into everything, including dessert — but in this mousse, it works like a charm. The crunchy topping adds a great texture to this smooth and creamy dessert, so it's not optional.
Serves 4-6

Mousse Ingredients

1½ cups vegan dark chocolate chips

1 (14-ounce) block silken tofu

⅓ cup maple syrup

⅓ cup chunky peanut butter

½ teaspoon vanilla extract

¼ teaspoon almond extract

¼ teaspoon ground cinnamon

Dash sea salt

Nut Topping

¼ cup evaporated cane sugar

1 cup toasted walnuts or pecan pieces

1 tablespoon neutral tasting oil

Dash ground cinnamon

Dash sea salt

Directions

Melt chocolate chips in a double boiler, or in a metal bowl over a small (2-quart) pot, filled with about 1 inch water. Let chocolate chips melt for about 3 minutes, then stir until all chips are melted. Remove from heat and set aside.

In a large blender or food processor, combine tofu, maple syrup, peanut butter, vanilla and almond extracts, cinnamon and sea salt. Blend until mixture is uniform and creamy. Transfer mousse mixture to a bowl and refrigerate for 2 hours, or overnight for a thick consistency.

For the topping: Add sugar, nuts, oil, cinnamon and sea salt to a food processor and pulse 7-10 times, or until well ground.

To serve, place a small amount of mousse into a dessert cup or bowl, and sprinkle with crunchy topping.

Note: Double check your chocolate chip ingredients if you are gluten-free, to be sure barley is not in the list.

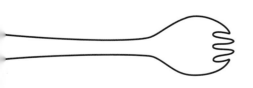

The Sporkie Scoop

FOR YOUR SMARTS Silken tofu has been eaten for thousands of years, and though we're using it in dessert, it's often enjoyed as a savory dish with just some spring onions and soy sauce.

FOR YOUR PARTS Cinnamon is amazing at warming the bod — and ladies, making cinnamon tea with a few cinnamon sticks in boiling water can help prevent the crampies and other symptoms of PMS.[43]

Cinnamon Sugar Churros

Making churros is an art form. A person who makes churros professionally is a *churrero*. Our recipe is a quick and easy version of this Spanish and Latin American treat. To be honest, it's a little too easy to make these churros, so use this recipe with caution because it's not our healthiest. Making these with a buddy is the way to go, because it helps the process go fast … and no one should eat churros solo. **Yields 20-25 three-inch churros**

Ingredients

¼ cup non-dairy butter

1 cup water

¼ teaspoon sea salt

2 tablespoons evaporated cane sugar, plus 1 cup

1 cup unbleached all-purpose flour

¼ teaspoon freshly grated nutmeg

¼ teaspoon ground cinnamon, plus 2 teaspoons

2 teaspoons egg replacer, dry, plus 1 tablespoon water

3 cups neutral tasting high-heat oil, for frying

Directions

In a small (2-quart) pot, heat butter and water together over medium heat until butter is melted. Add sea salt, and 2 tablespoons sugar, and stir until dissolved.

When mixture is boiling, add flour, nutmeg and ¼ teaspoon cinnamon. Stir well until mixture forms a ball of dough. Transfer to a large bowl.

Begin heating oil for frying in large (6-quart) pot.

Whisk egg replacer well with water and stir into dough.

In a separate shallow bowl or plate, combine remaining sugar with remaining cinnamon and set aside.

Place warm dough in a piping bag fitted with a large star tip. If you don't have a piping bag, roll churros into coils and cut them to desired length.

To fry churros: Test to see if oil is hot enough to fry by inserting a wooden tool. If bubbles form around the base of the tool, oil is ready for frying. Pipe churros into hot oil and cut with kitchen scissors to desired length.

Fry for about 2-3 minutes on each side to get a golden brown color.

Place fried churros on a paper towel-lined dish, and then roll each churro in cinnamon sugar mixture.

Serve warm.

The Sporkie Scoop

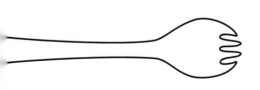

FOR YOUR SMARTS Churros were made popular in Latin America by way of Spain. They are usually eaten for breakfast, as a snack or as dessert—so you can always find the time to indulge with these treats.

FOR YOUR PARTS We don't fry often, but when we do, we make sure to use a high-heat oil like safflower or refined coconut. When an oil smokes, it becomes carcinogenic, so use high-heat oils for high-heat cooking.

Crispy Green Tea Cookies

Who can refuse a delicious crispy cookie? It goes so well with a glass of almond milk or a cup of tea, and you can create a whole different cookie experience by using alternatives to the green tea that we use below. Try using some Earl Grey for a more floral taste or some mint tea for a refreshing flavor. If you need a little more decadence, dip this cookie in some melted dark chocolate. **Yields about 18 cookies**

Ingredients

⅓ cup non-dairy butter

½ cup powdered sugar

½ teaspoon vanilla extract

2 tablespoons maple syrup

1 heaping tablespoon green tea leaves, finely ground (or 2 tea bags)

½ cup unbleached all-purpose flour, plus more for cutting board

½ cup spelt flour, or whole wheat pastry flour

⅛ teaspoon sea salt

Directions

Preheat oven to 350°F.

With a mixer or by hand, cream together the butter, sugar, vanilla extract and maple syrup.

With a mortar and pestle or coffee grinder, grind tea into fine powder. Add tea into mixture. Slowly incorporate flours and sea salt. Mix until dough is uniform. Do not overmix.

Place dough on a generously floured board and roll with rolling pin until about ⅛ inch thick. If dough sticks to cutting board or rolling pin, use more flour and rub it directly on board or rolling pin.

Using a cookie cutter of any shape, press into dough. Place formed cookies on a greased cookie sheet lined with parchment paper or a silicone baking mat (or use cooking spray).

Bake cookies for about 22-24 minutes, rotating halfway through. Bake until golden around edges.

Cool completely on a cooling rack and store in a metal tin for up to 2 weeks. Cookies stored in plastic will lose their crunch.

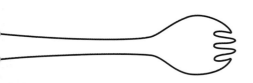

The Sporkie Scoop

FOR YOUR SMARTS So what is the diff between whole wheat pastry flour and regular whole wheat flour? Pastry flour is cut very fine and made from a soft wheat berry that is higher in carbs and lower in protein than the hard wheat used to make standard whole wheat flour. The result is a more delicate tasting flour, which makes it great for baked goodies!

FOR YOUR PARTS Both green and black tea come from the same little shrub. Green tea is a powerful cancer preventive because of its flavonoid content, and it is known to have more health benefits than black tea.[44]

Crunchy Peanut Butter Bonbons

When people take a bite of these bonbons, they experience a bite of crunchy, cold, peano-choco-ey deliciousness. The bread crumbs are the secret ingredient in this recipe, to add that candy bar effect. You'll feel like a kid in a candy store! This dessert is pretty quick and simple, and yields a lot of bonbons, so they are great to serve to a crowd. **Yields 16-20 bonbons**

Ingredients

¼ cup non-dairy butter

1½ cups powdered sugar

1 cup smooth peanut butter

1 cup organic unseasoned bread crumbs

¼ teaspoon ground cinnamon

¼ teaspoon sea salt

1 teaspoon vanilla extract

1 (12-ounce) package vegan dark chocolate chips

1 tablespoon neutral tasting oil

¼ cup ground peanuts, combined with 1 teaspoon sugar and ¼ teaspoon ground cinnamon (optional topping)

Directions

In a large bowl or standing mixer, combine butter, powdered sugar, peanut butter, bread crumbs, cinnamon, sea salt, and vanilla extract. Stir well, mixing until uniform.

Roll mixture into 1-inch balls and place on a cookie sheet lined with parchment paper or a silicone baking mat (or use cooking spray). Freeze until hard, about 20 minutes.

Meanwhile, create a double boiler by placing 1-2 inches of water in a small (2-quart) pot. Cover with a metal or heatproof glass bowl. Add chocolate chips and cook over medium heat until melted. Stir in oil and whisk until smooth.

Remove frozen peanut butter balls from freezer and dip each bonbon in melted chocolate, using a skewer or small fork.

Place dipped bonbons back on cookie sheet to firm up. If desired, top with additional dollop of chocolate or ground peanuts with sugar and cinnamon.

Freeze until ready to serve. Let bonbons sit at room temp for 5 minutes before serving.

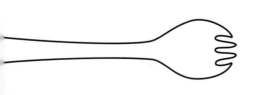

The Sporkie Scoop

FOR YOUR SMARTS   A bonbon is a piece of candy or sweets, dipped in chocolate. In French, *bon* means good, and we couldn't agree more. Go ahead and spell it bonbon, bon bon or bon-bon, and you will be right every time!

FOR YOUR PARTS   Medical research suggests that eating peanut butter, a niacin-rich food, can protect you against Alzheimer's disease![45]

Sopapillas with an Agave Cinnamon Drizzle

Sopapillas are eaten all over South America, but our favorite version is from New Mexico! You can eat them as a dessert, putting a little of the agave cinnamon drizzle inside each of the fluffy, doughy pillows—or you can even dip them in green or red chili sauce for a savory twist. There will be no honey needed for these sopapillas (check out "For Your Parts," below, to see why!).

Yields 8-10 large sopapillas

Drizzle Ingredients

¼ cup agave nectar

¼ cup brown rice syrup

¼ teaspoon sea salt

½ teaspoon ground cinnamon

Dash fresh lemon or lime juice

Sopapilla Ingredients

3 cups unbleached all-purpose flour, plus more for cutting board

¾ cup whole wheat pastry flour

2 teaspoons non-aluminum baking powder

1 teaspoon sea salt

1 teaspoon dry yeast, or ⅜ teaspoon active dry yeast.

3 tablespoons non-dairy butter

1¾ cups warm water

3-4 cups neutral tasting high-heat oil

2 teaspoons evaporated cane sugar (optional)

½ teaspoon cinnamon (optional)

Directions

For the agave cinnamon drizzle:
Combine agave, brown rice syrup, sea salt, cinnamon, and lemon or lime juice in a bowl, and set aside.

For the sopapillas: In a large bowl, add flours, baking powder and sea salt. Whisk to incorporate. Add yeast and whisk. Using a pastry cutter, add butter, incorporating until a "wet sand" consistency is reached.

Add warm water to mixture and knead dough until it forms a soft ball. Cover with a damp towel and let stand for 20-30 minutes.

Place additional all-purpose flour on a cutting board and roll out half the dough, keeping other half covered with a damp cloth. Roll until dough is about ⅛-¼ inch thick. Cut into 3-inch squares.

Heat oil in a large (6-quart) pot. Test to see if it's hot enough to fry by inserting a wooden tool. If bubbles form around the base of the tool, oil is ready for frying. Fry 1 or 2 squares at a time, until golden brown and puffed on both sides. Drain on paper towels.

Serve warm, drizzled with agave-cinnamon mixture. Sprinkle with sugar and additional cinnamon if desired.

The Sporkie Scoop

FOR YOUR SMARTS A sopapilla (pronounced soap-ah-PEE-ya) is a fried pastry or bread, and different varieties are served in many parts of South America, Mexico and the southwestern United States.

FOR YOUR PARTS So why don't your Sporkies eat honey? Much of our honey is produced by factory-farmed honeybees—and those practices (including using antibiotics, carbolic acid for the removal of honey, and calcium cyanide for killing colonies before extracting the honey) aren't gonna fly with us! We personally avoid honey, beeswax, propolis and royal jelly. Fight the power, and leave honey to the bees.

Strawberry Shortcakes with a Coconut Whipped Cream Topping

This recipe is pretty quick to put together and a lot of fun to eat, because it is a little messy. You can try serving these shortcakes with a spork and knife, but they should be considered finger food. If it's too hot outside to bake the biscuits, serving the whipped cream and berries as dessert ain't half bad either. And just a little word of warning: These shortcakes may look cute and innocent, but they're addictive. **Advance preparation required. Yields 6-7 individual shortcakes**

Strawberry Ingredients

2 cups fresh strawberries, sliced, plus more for garnish

⅓ cup evaporated cane sugar

1 teaspoon lemon juice, plus grated zest of ½ lemon

½ teaspoon vanilla extract

Shortcake Ingredients

2 cups unbleached all-purpose flour

1 tablespoon non-aluminum baking powder

1 tablespoon egg replacer, dry

2 tablespoons evaporated cane sugar

¼ teaspoon sea salt

⅓ cup non-dairy butter

¾ cup unsweetened almond or soymilk, plus 1 teaspoon unfiltered apple cider vinegar, curdled

2 tablespoons maple syrup, for brushing

Coconut Whipped Cream Ingredients

1 (14-ounce) can regular coconut milk (not light), refrigerated overnight

2 teaspoons maple syrup

¼ teaspoon sea salt

¼ teaspoon vanilla extract

Directions

Preheat oven to 425°F.

Toss together strawberries, sugar, lemon juice, zest and vanilla extract in a small bowl. Set aside.

For the shortcakes: In a medium bowl, combine flour, baking powder, egg replacer, sugar and sea salt. Use a pastry cutter to incorporate butter until mixture is coarse and crumbly. Create a well in center of dough and add curdled almond or soymilk. Stir until just combined. Do not over-mix.

On a floured cutting board, roll out dough, and use a biscuit cutter to cut out rounds. Place on baking sheet lined with parchment paper or a silicone baking mat (or use cooking spray), and brush with maple syrup.

Bake for 17-20 minutes, or until golden brown.

For the coconut whipped cream:

Refrigerating the can overnight allows the coconut cream to separate from the coconut water. So when you open it, hold the can steady and be careful not to shake it.

(continued on next page)

Strawberry Shortcakes with a Coconut Whipped Cream Topping

(continued from previous page)

Directions (continued)

With a spatula or spoon, remove only cream from top and discard coconut water. Place coconut cream, maple syrup, sea salt and vanilla extract in a standing mixer and mix on high for about 1 minute, or mix by hand by vigorously whisking for 4-5 minutes.

Let shortcakes cool partially and slice each in half horizontally, creating two layers, like a hamburger bun. Place a tablespoon of strawberries on bottom layer of biscuit. Dollop with coconut whipped cream and place "lid" portion of shortcake on top. Garnish with strawberries, if desired.

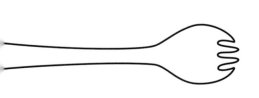

The Sporkie Scoop

FOR YOUR SMARTS You can make your own vanilla extract — yes, you can! All it takes is a bottle of vodka, some vanilla beans, and a little time! Slice a few beans lengthwise, throw them in that bottle, give it a shake or two, and let it hang out for about a month or longer (depending on the size of the bottle, it may need more time).

FOR YOUR PARTS Our love for coconut milk goes way beyond its incredible flavor. It is an immune-boosting food due to its anti-microbial, anti-viral and anti-fungal properties, which help your bod destroy all sorts of disease-causing organisms!

Cinnamon-Scented Tiramisu

The name tiramisu comes from the Italian phrase for "pick me up," because with all the chocolate, booze and coffee in this dessert, you really do get a good energy boost. This is no alternative to a protein shake or some trail mix before a workout, but once in a while it's okay to get a little buzz off a great dessert! Part of the beauty of tiramisu is the advance prep, so keep that in mind when creating this recipe. **Advance preparation and chilling time required. Serves 6-8 (photo on p. 149)**

Cake Ingredients

1 cup unbleached all-purpose flour

½ cup whole wheat pastry flour

1 teaspoon non-aluminum baking powder

½ teaspoon sea salt

½ teaspoon ground cinnamon

1 teaspoon vanilla extract

½ cup evaporated cane sugar

¾ cup unsweetened almond or soymilk, plus 1 teaspoon unfiltered apple cider vinegar, curdled

¼ cup neutral tasting oil

Creamy Topping Ingredients

1 tablespoon non-dairy butter

3 tablespoons evaporated cane sugar, plus 2 tablespoons

2 (8-ounce) containers vegan cream cheese

3 tablespoons regular coconut milk

2 teaspoons fresh lemon juice

2 teaspoons fresh orange juice

Dash sea salt

2 cups brewed coffee or espresso

¼ cup amaretto liqueur

½ cup vegan mini dark chocolate chips, or shaved dark chocolate

Directions

Preheat oven to 350°F.

In a medium bowl, whisk flours, baking powder, sea salt, cinnamon, vanilla extract and sugar until uniform. Add curdled almond or soymilk and oil.

Grease an 8 x 8 baking dish with cooking spray and pour in batter. Bake for 20-25 minutes, or until toothpick comes out clean when inserted into the middle of cake. Allow to cool.

For the topping: In a small (2-quart) pot, melt butter and 3 tablespoons sugar over low heat. Cook for about 2-3 minutes, until a caramel forms and sugar looks dissolved.

(continued on next page)

Cinnamon-Scented Tiramisu

(continued from previous page)

Directions (continued)

In the bowl of a standing mixer or by hand, whisk together cream cheese and coconut milk on high for about 30 seconds, or until well blended. Add caramelized sugar, lemon juice, orange juice and sea salt. Blend for additional 30-60 seconds. Refrigerate cream for 30 minutes to overnight, allowing flavors to develop.

Combine coffee or espresso in a medium bowl with amaretto and 2 tablespoons sugar.

Slice cooled cake into long, inch-thick strips and place in a 9 x 12 baking dish. Pour coffee and amaretto mixture over cake and let rest for about 1 hour.

To assemble: Begin with a layer of cake (either in individual serving cups or on one large serving dish). Top with layer of creamy topping. Repeat with additional cake layer, and additional creamy topping layer. Then top with chocolate chips or shaved chocolate.

Refrigerate overnight (8-12 hours) before serving for best results.

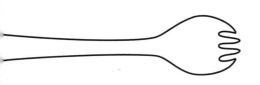

The Sporkie Scoop

FOR YOUR SMARTS Amaretto is an almond-flavored liqueur that is sometimes made with bitter almond pits, but it's mostly made with apricot pits! It didn't become popular in the United States until the 1960s, but now it is a familiar addition to many cocktails and baked treats. Don't be duped by a drink labeled "crème de almond," because it isn't real amaretto!

FOR YOUR PARTS If you are feeling overheated in the oppressive summer heat or after a strenuous workout—eat an orange! Oranges can help cool the bod, proving that soccer moms everywhere really know their stuff.[46]

Vanilla Birthday Cake with a Buttercream Frosting and Sprinkles

Put on your ridiculous birthday hat, preheat the oven and treat yourself or anyone you love to this light and fluffy vanilla cake. There is a time for sophisticated cuisine, but on your b-day you want comfort and fun—which is where this cake fits in! You'll feel like a kid when you sneak your finger into the buttercream frosting when no one is peeking. And you can't get in trouble, because it's your birthday! **Serves 6-8**

Ingredients

1 cup spelt flour

1 cup unbleached all-purpose flour

1 teaspoon non-aluminum baking powder

1 teaspoon baking soda

2 teaspoons egg replacer, dry

½ teaspoon sea salt

2 cups unsweetened almond or soymilk, plus 1½ teaspoons unfiltered apple cider vinegar, curdled

⅓ cup neutral tasting oil

1 cup evaporated cane sugar

1 tablespoon vanilla extract

3 tablespoons naturally dyed sprinkles

Frosting Ingredients

⅓ cup non-dairy butter

4-4½ cups powdered sugar

1 teaspoon vanilla extract

Dash sea salt

2 tablespoons unsweetened almond or soymilk

Directions

Preheat oven to 350°F.

In a large bowl, combine flours, baking powder, baking soda, egg replacer and sea salt. Whisk until uniform.

In a separate bowl, whisk curdled almond or soymilk, oil, sugar and vanilla extract, and slowly incorporate into dry ingredients. Mix batter until uniform, but do not overmix.

Pour batter into two greased 9-inch-round baking dishes. Bake for about 20 minutes, or until a toothpick comes out clean when inserted into middle of cake.

For the frosting: Leave butter on counter for about 30 minutes to soften before using. To whip, place butter, powdered sugar, vanilla extract, sea salt, and almond or soymilk in a mixing bowl and whisk by hand, or in a standing mixer with a whisk attachment.

To assemble: Let cake rounds cool completely. Trim with bread knife if tops are uneven. Place first cake round on a large surface that rotates, or on a cake plate. Spread an even ¼-inch layer of frosting on cake round, using a flat spatula. Refrigerate for about 20 minutes for best consistency. Place second cake round on top of first, and frost entire cake from top down. Scatter sprinkles over the top.

The Sporkie Scoop

FOR YOUR SMARTS Baking powder and baking soda are used as quick leaveners instead of yeast, which takes a while. In general, they help fluff up your baked goodies by releasing CO_2, which becomes thousands of bubbles of air in batter or dough.

FOR YOUR PARTS We never use bleached flour, not even on our birthdays! The reason is that bleached flour is treated with nasty chemicals, like benzoyl peroxide or chlorine gas, so it becomes whiter, more shelf-stable and produces longer chains of gluten to yield more uniform baked goods. This process is shunned in Europe—and by us, because it's unnecessary and it just ain't right![47]

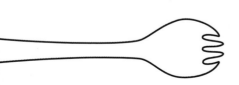

Peanut Butter Oatmeal Chocolate Chip Cookies

These crunchy peanut buttery little gems are crazy good. No one will know or care that they're vegan because they'll be busy stuffing their faces and asking for more. When they sing your praises, raising a glass of almond milk to you, go ahead and take all the credit — we're sharing the love. **Yields about 16 cookies**

Ingredients

½ cup non-dairy butter

¾ cup evaporated cane sugar

½ teaspoon vanilla extract

2 heaping tablespoons smooth peanut butter

2 tablespoons maple syrup

⅛ teaspoon sea salt

2 teaspoons egg replacer, dry

½ teaspoon ground cinnamon

¾ cup unbleached all-purpose flour

¾ cup rolled oats

¼ cup vegan dark chocolate chips

Directions

Preheat oven to 350°F.

In a large bowl or bowl of a standing mixer, cream butter and sugar until well mixed and soft. Add vanilla extract, peanut butter, maple syrup, sea salt, egg replacer and cinnamon. Mix until all ingredients are uniform.

Add flour and oats. Mix until all ingredients look evenly distributed. Fold in chocolate chips.

Line a cookie sheet with parchment paper or a silicone baking mat (or use cooking spray). Scoop the dough with a tablespoon for even-sized cookies. Place about 1 inch apart.

Bake for about 15-18 minutes, rotating cookie sheets halfway through. Bake until edges are golden-brown.

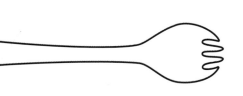

The Sporkie Scoop

FOR YOUR SMARTS The ancient Mayans and Aztecs inspired the PB we love today! They used roasted peanuts and made them into a paste — simple and delish.

FOR YOUR PARTS Men and maple — you love each other. Here's one reason why: Maple syrup is high in zinc and manganese, which can help promote prostate health!

Crème Fraîche and Berry Parfait (gf)

Let's face it—sometimes you need a little sweet fix. We keep cans of coconut milk in the fridge at all times, and you should, too. Having dinner parties is our favorite thing in the world, and when you throw a last-minute shindig, this is the recipe to bust out. It only takes a few minutes (provided you have followed our advice and don't mess around) and it's so good your guests might just toss off a profanity or two. **Advance preparation required. Serves 4-6**

Ingredients

2 (14-ounce) cans regular coconut milk, pre-chilled (see directions)

1 tablespoon non-dairy butter

3 tablespoons evaporated cane sugar

1 teaspoon fresh lemon juice

1-2 teaspoons fresh orange juice

Dash vanilla extract

Dash sea salt

1 pint fresh strawberries, sliced

1 pint fresh blueberries

Directions

Refrigerate 2 cans of coconut milk for 24 hours before using.

In a small (2-quart) pot, melt butter and sugar over low heat. Cook for about 2-3 minutes to caramelize sugar, stirring constantly until sugar has dissolved and your mixture is smooth and uniform. Remove from heat and set aside.

Carefully open pre-chilled cans of coconut milk and remove firm, white coconut cream layer from top, avoiding the coconut water. Only the cream will be used. In a mixer, whisk coconut cream on high for about 30 seconds, or until well blended. Add caramelized sugar, lemon juice, orange juice, vanilla extract and sea salt. Blend for an additional 30-60 seconds.

To serve, layer berries and crème fraîche in individual glasses, or large clear bowl.

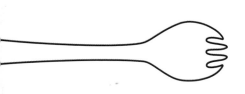

The Sporkie Scoop

FOR YOUR SMARTS Strawberries aren't in fact a true berry! This delish imposter is actually a member of the rose family. And here's a mindblower—they can have over 200 seeds per strawb!

FOR YOUR PARTS Bluebs have the same bacteria-fighting powers as cranberries. (Gentlemen, close your eyes.) These suckers can really knock out a UTI! And they taste great on their own … no sugar needed![48]

Pumpkin Cheesecake with a Gingersnap Crust

Sometimes in spring or summer we wish that it was fall, just so we could make this pumpkin cheesecake! The crust is so gingery and snappy and the filling is so good, you can eat it on its own. Of course you can serve this at any holiday gathering with pride. It is especially handy because you create it in advance, giving you time to be social—and explain to your friends and fam why you don't need cheese in cheesecake. **Chilling time required. Serves 8-10**

Crust Ingredients

1½ cups organic vegan gingersnap cookies (about 24 cookies)

¼ cup almonds, toasted

2 teaspoons fresh ginger, grated

2 tablespoons neutral tasting oil

¼ cup brown or palm sugar

¼ teaspoon ground cinnamon

1 teaspoon vanilla extract

½ teaspoon sea salt

Pumpkin Filling Ingredients

2 (8-ounce) containers vegan cream cheese

⅓ cup evaporated cane sugar

1 (15-ounce) can organic pumpkin

¼ teaspoon ground cloves

¼ teaspoon freshly grated nutmeg

¼ teaspoon ground allspice

½ teaspoon ground cinnamon

1 tablespoon whole wheat pastry flour

1 tablespoon fresh lemon juice

1 tablespoon neutral tasting oil

⅛ teaspoon sea salt

Directions

Preheat oven to 350°F.

For the crust: Place cookies, almonds, ginger, oil, sugar, cinnamon, vanilla extract and sea salt in a food processor and pulse until uniform, about 20-25 times. Mixture should be a crumbly, even consistency that pulls away from walls of food processor.

Grease a springform pan. Use damp hands to firmly press mixture into pan to form crust. Be sure to evenly distribute mixture and use thumbs to press crust into corners of pan. Bake for 7 minutes, to help crust stick together.

For the filling: In a food processor, combine cream cheese, sugar, pumpkin, cloves, nutmeg, allspice, cinnamon, flour, lemon juice, oil and sea salt. Blend until uniform.

Pour filling into baked crust and gently tap mixture on counter to release any trapped bubbles. Bake for about 40 minutes or until mixture is slightly browned on top and feels firm when pan is slightly shaken.

Remove from oven and allow cheesecake to cool on counter for at least 20 minutes, then refrigerate for 4 hours to overnight before serving, to firm up.

The Sporkie Scoop

FOR YOUR SMARTS At some point in your life you may cut into a piece of ginger and see a blue-greenish ring of color inside! Let us congratulate you, you just scored a Hawaiian variety of ginger called (you guessed it) blue-ringed ginger! The flavor and texture are extraordinary. Use it just like you would use any other variety.

FOR YOUR PARTS About 99% of pumpkins in the United States are used for Halloween jack-o-lanterns, but that's not all they're good for! These winter squash have been used to treat bronchial asthma, as they can help dispel all sorts of nasty things from your lungs and throat.[49]

Chocolate Mint Truffles (gf optional)

This is the best dessert to make in advance if you are in the mood for some serious chocolate! The cooling touch of mint balances out the richness of the dark chocolate, making these pretty darn delish. If you have any kids in the house, have them pitch in when rolling these precious treats, because your hands get chocolatey and it's a good time for all. Instead of rolling these in cocoa powder, you can try using toasted finely shredded coconut, chopped almonds or organic powdered sugar!
Advance preparation required. Yields 13-15 truffles

Ingredients

1½ cups vegan dark chocolate chips
½ cup regular coconut milk
1 teaspoon peppermint extract
6 leaves fresh mint, finely chopped
Dash sea salt
2 tablespoons organic cocoa powder, plus ¼ cup for rolling

Directions

Fill a small (2-quart) pot with about 2 inches of water, and bring to a simmer over medium heat. Place a glass or metal bowl on top of pot to create a double boiler.

Add chocolate chips and melt, about 3-4 minutes. Add coconut milk, peppermint extract, mint, sea salt and 2 tablespoons cocoa powder, and incorporate until uniform.

Transfer mixture to a bowl and refrigerate 2 hours to overnight. Remove from refrigerator and leave bowl on counter for 5-10 minutes to soften mixture before rolling truffles.

To roll truffles: Place remaining cocoa powder in a shallow bowl or plate. Use a melon baller or spoon to scoop a gumball-size dollop of the chocolate mixture. Roll into balls between palms and immediately coat in cocoa powder, or other toppings of choice.

Note 1: Try using mint varieties like chocolate mint, peppermint or spearmint for a different flavor in these truffles, and choose organic when possible, because conventionally grown mint is sprayed with a bunch of pesticides!

Note 2: Double check your chocolate chip ingredients if you are gluten-free, to be sure barley is not in the list.

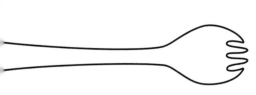

The Sporkie Scoop

FOR YOUR SMARTS With these truffles, you are getting a double dose of antioxidants. We're using cocoa powder inside and outside the truffles. Cocoa powder is about 8% antioxidants by weight—so that's more than a glass of wine or cup of tea!

FOR YOUR PARTS Mint doesn't just taste refreshing, it's actually working to soothe your stomach and digestion. It's considered a powerful digestive aid and anti-spasmotic because of its antioxidant-rich oils.[50]

BRUNCH

*(gf) indicates the recipe is gluten-free!

Sticky Maple Pecan Cinnamon Rolls

This is not a quick breakfast treat, so don't make these if you are expecting instant gratification. It takes a little time and preparation to create these gooey, sticky cinnamon rolls, but it is definitely worth the effort! When you're baking them, you will make the whole house smell amazing, and you won't need to wear perfume for the rest of the day, because you'll smell good, too. After all, the scent of cinnamon is a known aphrodisiac. **Advance preparation required. Yields 12-14 rolls**

Dough Ingredients

1 package (¼-ounce) active dry yeast or 2¼ teaspoons dry yeast

3 tablespoons warm water

1 cup unsweetened almond or soymilk

2 tablespoons non-dairy butter

2 cups unbleached all-purpose flour

1 cup whole wheat pastry flour

1 tablespoon, plus 1 teaspoon vital wheat gluten flour

1 tablespoon evaporated cane sugar

½ teaspoon sea salt

2 teaspoons neutral tasting oil

Filling Ingredients

¼ cup evaporated cane sugar

1 cup toasted pecan pieces

2 teaspoons neutral tasting oil

½ teaspoon ground cinnamon

Dash freshly grated nutmeg

¼ teaspoon sea salt

2 tablespoons non-dairy butter

Frosting Ingredients

¾ cup powdered sugar

1 tablespoon soy creamer

1 teaspoon maple syrup

1 teaspoon vanilla extract

Dash sea salt

Directions

For the dough: In a small glass bowl, combine yeast and warm water. Let yeast bloom for about 10 minutes without stirring.

In a small (2-quart) pot, heat almond or soymilk and butter until just warm to the touch, but not at a simmer.

In a large mixing bowl, whisk together flours, sugar and sea salt.

Add warm almond milk mixture and yeast mixture, and gently stir with a wooden spoon until dough forms a ball.

On a floured surface, knead dough by hand until smooth and elastic, about 7-10 minutes. If using a standing mixer, knead for about 3 minutes. Place dough in a clean large glass bowl, and coat in 2 teaspoons oil. Cover with a damp cloth and let rise on a countertop until doubled in size, about 1-1½ hours.

For the filling: In a food processor, pulse sugar, pecans, oil, cinnamon, nutmeg and sea salt about 15 times, or until finely ground. Set aside.

Preheat oven to 350°F.

(continued on next page)

Sticky Maple Pecan Cinnamon Rolls

(continued from previous page)

Directions (continued)

Heat a small (2-quart) pot and melt butter over low-medium heat.

Brush rectangle of dough with most of melted butter. Sprinkle filling mixture evenly across entire surface. Roll rectangle along long horizontal edge into a coil. Cut into 2-inch rounds. Place rounds, swirl side up, on a baking sheet lined with parchment paper or a silicone baking mat (or use cooking spray).

Cover rolls and allow to rise until almost doubled in size, about 30 minutes. Brush rolls lightly with remaining melted butter. Bake for 30 minutes or until golden brown.

For the frosting: Whisk powdered sugar, creamer, maple syrup, vanilla extract and sea salt together until mixture is smooth. Generously drizzle over cooled cinnamon rolls.

Note: Yeast and metal don't get along, so use glass or other types of bowls when making these!

The Sporkie Scoop

FOR YOUR SMARTS A cinnamon roll you can buy at the mall in a food court will pack you with about 880 calories! Our rolls come with all the flavor, none of the cholesterol — and are around 200 cals!

FOR YOUR PARTS So why is cinnamon an aphrodisiac food?! It gets your circulation going — and that's what gets your blood pumping, if you know what we mean![51]

Strawberry Cream Cheese-Stuffed French Toast

You can make this extraordinary brunch dish in 10 minutes flat, even if you had a few too many drinkies the night before! Using simple ingredients that are in every well-stocked kitchen, and flour as our binder, we whisk it, dip it, cook it and eat it. You can serve this to your lovey as breakfast in bed, because before he or she can wake up and smell this cooking, it'll be done!
Serves 4-6 (photo on p. 167)

Batter Ingredients

¾ cup spelt flour

¼ cup unbleached all-purpose flour

1 teaspoon non-aluminum baking powder

½ teaspoon sea salt

½ teaspoon ground cinnamon

¼ teaspoon ground allspice

2 tablespoons maple syrup

1 teaspoon vanilla extract

½ teaspoon almond extract

1 ⅓ cups unsweetened almond or soymilk

Grated zest of 1 lemon

2 tablespoons neutral tasting high-heat oil, plus additional for coating the pan

Strawberry Cream Cheese Ingredients

1 container vegan cream cheese

4-5 strawberries, finely chopped

2 tablespoons brown rice syrup

¼ teaspoon ground cinnamon

¼ teaspoon sea salt

½ teaspoon vanilla extract

Dash fresh lemon juice

8-10 strawberries, sliced

1 large spelt boule or French bread

Directions

For the batter: In a medium bowl, whisk together flours, baking powder, sea salt, cinnamon and allspice. Add in the maple syrup, vanilla and almond extracts, almond or soymilk, lemon zest and 2 tablespoons oil. Whisk until smooth. Do not overmix.

For the cream cheese: In a separate large bowl, combine cream cheese and strawberries. Add brown rice syrup, cinnamon, sea salt, vanilla extract and lemon juice, and whisk with a fork to combine.

Place sliced strawberries in a bowl.

Slice boule or loaf into large 2-inch-thick slices, and cut into each slice horizontally to form a pocket— but don't cut all the way through bread.

(continued on next page)

Strawberry Cream Cheese-Stuffed French Toast

(continued from previous page)

Directions (continued)

Preheat griddle or pan to medium-high heat. Grease with additional oil.

Stuff each slice of bread with strawberry cream cheese and a few slices of strawberries. Coat each bread slice in batter, and then place on griddle or hot pan.

Cook until bottom becomes slightly golden and edges look dry, about 2-3 minutes. Flip and cook for another 2-3 minutes, or until golden. Let French toast cool for about 3 minutes before cutting. Slice in half with a diagonal cut for best presentation.

The Sporkie Scoop

FOR YOUR SMARTS   What do you do when you are in France and your bread has been around for a day or two? You make French toast, known in France as *pain perdu*, meaning lost bread, because dipping tough bread into a coating and frying it on both sides brings this baby to life!

FOR YOUR PARTS   Spelt flour, a cousin of wheat, is an ancient grain that has a sturdier outer hull that protects it from pests and pollutants. Because of this, you can get a non-organic variety that is still going to be super health supportive! It also digests like a dream, so eat up!

Chive and Cheddar Skillet Omelet (gf)

We created this omelet because we wanted the tastes and flavors that we had before our vegan days. Omelets are a breakfast staple for many people, and this dish is just as simple as its ovo-heavy counterpart. You can whip it up in no time and use it as a base for your veganized favorites of classics like the Denver omelet, the hang-town fry or anything else you can think up!

Serves 6-8

Ingredients

1 (14-ounce) block firm tofu, pressed and drained (see recipe for homemade tofu on p. 84)

¼ cup unsweetened almond or soymilk

2 teaspoons non-aluminum baking powder

1 tablespoon egg replacer, dry

2 tablespoons gluten-free all-purpose flour

2 tablespoons arrowroot powder

2 tablespoons nutritional yeast flakes

1 tablespoon brown rice syrup

1 teaspoon sea salt

¼ teaspoon finely ground black pepper

½ teaspoon turmeric

1 tablespoon neutral tasting oil

1 tablespoon light miso paste (non-barley)

3 tablespoons fresh lemon juice

1 tablespoon neutral tasting high-heat oil, for greasing pan

½ cup shredded vegan cheddar cheese

5-8 leaves fresh basil, finely chopped

1 bunch fresh chives, finely chopped

Directions

Preheat broiler to high.

In food processor combine tofu, almond or soymilk, baking powder, egg replacer, flour, arrowroot powder, nutritional yeast, brown rice syrup, sea salt, black pepper, turmeric, oil, miso and lemon juice. Blend until mixture is uniform and smooth.

Grease an oven-proof non-stick sauté pan generously with high-heat oil. Place tofu mixture into pan, and spread out evenly. Cook over low heat, covered, for about 5 minutes without stirring.

Remove lid and continue to cook over medium heat for an additional 3-5 minutes.

Sprinkle omelet with vegan cheese. Place sauté pan in oven and broil for 3 minutes, or until browned. Top with basil and chives. Let cool for 5-10 minutes, and transfer to a platter. Serve warm.

The Sporkie Scoop

FOR YOUR SMARTS Chives aren't just a garnish, they're beneficial to plant in your garden! If you plant chives near rose bushes, their odor discourages aphids!

FOR YOUR PARTS Nutritional yeast is high in viteys and minerals, including chromium, which is great for regulating blood sugar levels. To get the most from your nutritional yeast, check to see if it has B-12, an important nutrient to supplement when you are veeg.[52]

Smoky Tempeh Bacon, Broccoli and Cheese Quiche

Quiche is a dish that is fun to make not only for brunch, but any time of day. This recipe can be adapted to suit any genre, so if you are going for a more Southwest vibe, replace the tempeh bacon and broccoli with some black beans and corn. It's also really good cold. If you have leftovers, don't worry – they won't go to waste. **Serves 8**

Crust Ingredients

1 cup unbleached all-purpose flour

½ cup finely ground yellow cornmeal

1 teaspoon sea salt

½ teaspoon non-aluminum baking powder

⅓ cup neutral tasting oil

1 tablespoon egg replacer, dry

1 teaspoon dried oregano

1 tablespoon mustard, stone ground or German

1 tablespoon agave nectar

1 tablespoon cold water, plus more if needed

Filling Ingredients

2 teaspoons non-dairy butter

2 heads broccoli, coarsely chopped

5-7 strips tempeh bacon

2 cloves garlic, minced

¼ teaspoon sea salt, plus ½ teaspoon

¼ teaspoon finely ground black pepper, plus ½ teaspoon

1 (14-ounce) block firm tofu, pressed and drained (see recipe for homemade tofu on p. 84)

1 teaspoon non-aluminum baking powder

2 teaspoons egg replacer, dry

1 tablespoon neutral tasting oil

2 teaspoons agave nectar

½ teaspoon turmeric

1 teaspoon vegan Worcestershire sauce

1 teaspoon light miso paste

1 tablespoon fresh lemon juice

¼ cup shredded vegan cheddar cheese

Directions

Preheat oven to 375°F.

For the crust: Combine flour, cornmeal, sea salt and baking powder in a large bowl. Using a pastry cutter, incorporate oil, egg replacer, oregano, mustard, agave and cold water, until uniform and dough holds together. Overworking dough makes it tough, not flaky.

Grease a tart pan and press crust into edges first, and then center of pan. Poke dough with a fork. Bake empty for 8-10 minutes.

For the filling: In a large sauté pan with high sides, melt the butter. Add broccoli, tempeh bacon, garlic, and ¼ teaspoon each of sea salt and black pepper, and cook over low heat until browned. Set aside.

(continued on next page)

Smoky Tempeh Bacon, Broccoli and Cheese Quiche

(continued from previous page)

Directions (continued)

In a food processor, combine tofu, baking powder, egg replacer, oil, agave, remaining sea salt and black pepper, turmeric, Worcestershire sauce, miso and lemon juice. Mix until filling is uniform and smooth. Fold in broccoli-tempeh mixture and cheese.

Pour filling into baked crust and bake for about 40-50 minutes, or until filling is firm and slightly browned. Serve warm.

The Sporkie Scoop

FOR YOUR SMARTS Quiche originated in Europe and has become a staple of French cuisine. Our quiche uses a tofu base instead of cream and eggs, so don't feel guilty if you want to snag an extra bite or two.

FOR YOUR PARTS Broccoli is not just an amazing cancer fighter, packed with tons of viteys—it can also help cure pinkeye! Make a little broc and carrot tea to fight off this pesky eye condition.[53]

Sweet Potato Biscuits and Gravy

Biscuits and gravy are an insanely good Southern breakfast or brunch delicacy. We were once traumatized when we saw a crossword puzzle clue that said, "what a vegan eats for breakfast" and the answer was "muesli," so we do our best to shake things up a bit. **Yields 12-14 biscuits** (photo on p. 175)

Biscuit Ingredients

1 cup cooked sweet potatoes, peeled and cooled

½ cup non-dairy butter

1 cup unbleached all-purpose flour, plus extra for rolling the dough

1½ cups spelt flour

1 tablespoon non-aluminum baking powder

½ teaspoon dried thyme

1 teaspoon sea salt

½ teaspoon finely ground black pepper

½ teaspoon garlic powder

2 tablespoons lemon juice

½ cup soymilk creamer

Gravy Ingredients

¼ cup non-dairy butter

¼ cup unbleached all-purpose flour, plus extra for rolling the dough

2 vegan sausages, chopped

½ small white onion, finely chopped

2 cloves fresh garlic, finely chopped

1½ cups unsweetened almond or soymilk

1 cup soymilk creamer

½ teaspoon sea salt

½ teaspoon finely ground black pepper

1 bay leaf

Dash freshly grated nutmeg

Directions

Preheat oven to 425°F. If using a pizza stone, preheat in oven.

In a large bowl, combine sweet potato and butter with a potato masher or pastry whisk. Slowly add flours, baking powder, thyme, sea salt, black pepper and garlic powder. Whisk until uniform.

Add lemon juice and creamer to bowl with sweet potato mixture. Combine just until mixture holds together, being sure not to overwork dough. Roll out onto a floured surface to about ½-inch thickness and cut into rounds using a biscuit cutter or rim of a floured glass.

(continued on next page)

Directions (continued)

Place on a lightly oiled cookie sheet or pizza stone and bake for about 15 minutes.

For the gravy: Heat a medium (4-quart) pot over medium heat and add butter and flour. Whisk to create a roux. Add sausage, onion and garlic. Cook until browned. Add almond or soymilk, creamer, sea salt, black pepper, bay leaf and nutmeg. Cook until thick, stirring occasionally, about 10 minutes. Discard bay leaf.

Serve biscuits warm and slather with gravy.

The Sporkie Scoop

FOR YOUR SMARTS   There are a few different colors of peppercorns! Black, green and white are all the same type of what is considered to be a fruit, but are at varying stages of ripeness! Green is the least ripe, black is a bit more ripe, and white is fully mature — and the spiciest!

FOR YOUR PARTS   Living in a big city, breathing in all sorts of interesting things? Us, too! Luckily we eat sweet potatoes, which can strengthen and protect your lung tissue, due to their high vitamin A content![54]

Toasted Pecan Spelt Coffee Cake

Coffee cakes are often under-appreciated. They are so surprisingly good every time you eat them and they are appropriate both at brunch and dessert time — lucky little cake. Making a coffee cake is a great excuse to have friends or fam over and sit and chat a while. This coffee cake is so good your guests may never want to leave, so be careful whom you bake this for! **Serves 6-8**

Cake Ingredients

¾ cup non-dairy butter, at room temperature

⅔ cup evaporated cane sugar

2 tablespoons maple syrup

1 cup vegan sour cream

1 teaspoon vanilla extract

1 cup unbleached all-purpose flour

½ cup spelt flour

2 teaspoons baking powder

½ teaspoon baking soda

¼ teaspoon sea salt

1 tablespoon egg replacer, dry

1 teaspoon unfiltered apple cider vinegar

Topping Ingredients

¼ cup evaporated cane sugar

½ cup toasted pecans

2 tablespoons non-dairy butter

2 tablespoons spelt flour

¼ teaspoon ground cinnamon

Dash sea salt

Glaze Ingredients (optional)

½ cup powdered sugar

1-2 teaspoons unsweetened almond or soymilk

Directions

Preheat oven to 350°F.

In a large mixing bowl or bowl of a standing mixer, cream together butter and sugar. Add maple syrup, sour cream and vanilla extract, and whisk until uniform.

In a separate large bowl, combine flours, baking powder, baking soda, sea salt and egg replacer. Whisk to incorporate all ingredients.

Add liquid mixture and vinegar to dry ingredients, and whisk until smooth.

For the topping: Pulse sugar, pecans, butter, spelt flour, cinnamon and sea salt in a food processor until finely chopped. Set aside.

Spread batter in greased angel food pan or 8 x 8 baking dish. Sprinkle topping evenly over batter. Bake for 30-35 minutes, or until a toothpick comes out clean when inserted into middle of batter.

For the optional glaze: Whisk powdered sugar and almond or soymilk until smooth. Drizzle over cooled coffee cake.

The Sporkie Scoop

FOR YOUR SMARTS Pecans have a rich history in North America, as they helped sustain ancient Native American populations! A Spanish explorer named Cabeza de Vaca documented their relationship in the mid-1500s, writing about the Native Americans gathering pecans in autumn, soaking them in water, and making a milky drink. Not so far off from the nut milks we make at home!

FOR YOUR PARTS Do yourself (and us) a favor, and use only sea salt that hasn't been chemically bleached! Sodium is an essential mineral that we need to maintain proper water and electrolyte balance in our bods, and it brings out the flavors in our cooking. So throw out any bleached salts and replace them with unrefined sea salt! The ingredients should just be sea salt, no anti-caking agents allowed![55]

Tempeh Bacon-Stuffed Potato Pom Poms

Fried potatoes for brunch — yes, please (but not very often)! When you need to indulge and have fun with your brunch party, do it right by making these potato-ey gems! These homespun little tots are a bit too easy to make, so use this recipe with caution!

Yields about 24 pom poms

Ingredients

4 medium organic russet potatoes

¼ cup spelt flour

½ teaspoon garlic powder

Dash freshly grated nutmeg

1 teaspoon sea salt

½ teaspoon finely ground black pepper

¼ teaspoon cayenne pepper

1 cup neutral tasting high-heat oil for frying, plus 2 teaspoons for sautéeing

1 package tempeh bacon, finely chopped

Directions

Place grating attachment in food processor and grate potatoes. Place potatoes in a strainer lined with cheesecloth and press liquid out of potatoes, allowing to drain for about 15 minutes. Discard liquid.

Transfer grated potatoes to a large bowl. Add spelt flour, garlic powder, nutmeg, sea salt, black pepper and cayenne pepper. Stir together until thoroughly mixed.

Heat 1 cup oil in large (6-quart) pot. Test to see if it's hot enough to fry by inserting a wooden tool. If bubbles form around the base of the tool, oil is ready for frying.

Meanwhile, in a separate sauté pan, add chopped tempeh bacon and 2 teaspoons oil. Sauté until fragrant, about 3 minutes. Set aside.

To form pom poms, scoop about ¼ cup potato mixture and form into a bowl shape in your hand. Add about ½ teaspoon tempeh bacon to center and form into a small oval shape.

Carefully add pom poms to hot oil and cook for about 2 minutes on each side, until golden and crisp.

The Sporkie Scoop

FOR YOUR SMARTS Meet the granddaddy of our pom poms: What did people do before the Tater Tot was invented in 1953? We're not sure. But the folks at Ore-Ida are the creators of this (not-so-good-for-you) addictive treat and we have them to thank for our freshman 15 … and for our pom poms.

FOR YOUR PARTS In small amounts, like a pinch or two, nutmeg is quite good for you. It has strong anti-bacterial properties and has been shown to reduce cavity-causing bacteria in ya mouth. But in large amounts, nutmeg is toxic! Yes, 2 whole nutmegs can kill a person, putting a damper on your brunch plans.[56]

Lemon Ginger Scones with Crystallized Ginger

Scones have a rep for being a bit on the dry side, but this little brunch treat wants to be fluffy and moist, just like its muffin friends. The flavors of ginger and lemon are so fresh, they will help wake you up and get you going for the day! Serving these with a cup of tea or a cold glass of almond milk will enhance anyone's morning. **Yields 8-10 scones**

Ingredients

1½ cups unbleached all-purpose flour

1 cup spelt flour

⅓ cup evaporated cane sugar, plus 2 tablespoons for topping

2 teaspoons egg replacer, dry

½ teaspoon sea salt

1 tablespoon plus 1 teaspoon non-aluminum baking powder

¾ cup non-dairy butter

½ teaspoon vanilla extract

½ cup unsweetened almond or soymilk

¼ cup fresh lemon juice

1 teaspoon grated lemon zest (optional)

1 tablespoon grated ginger

4-5 pieces crystallized ginger, finely chopped (about 2 tablespoons)

Directions

Preheat oven to 425°F.

In a large bowl combine flours, ⅓ cup sugar, egg replacer, sea salt and baking powder. Mix to incorporate ingredients.

Add butter to mixture by cutting it in with a pastry whisk until mixture appears crumbly.

Add vanilla extract, almond or soymilk, lemon juice and zest, if using, and grated ginger. Mix until just incorporated. Add crystallized ginger pieces. Dough will not be completely smooth.

Gather dough into a ball and place on a lightly floured surface. Roll dough into a ½-inch-thick square. Cut into 2-inch strips, then cut into squares and slice each square diagonally to make a triangle. Place triangles on greased baking sheet and sprinkle with cinnamon sugar.

Bake for about 15 minutes, or until golden brown.

The Sporkie Scoop

FOR YOUR SMARTS Scotland is considered the land where scones originated, and we're so happy they came up with this treat! You can create savory scones by substituting some of the ginger and sugar with ingredients such as vegan cheese or dill.[57]

FOR YOUR PARTS If you are prone to getting motion sickness, then ginger is your saving grace. It helps settle tummy upset or nausea associated with motion sickness and has even been known to prevent the up-chucks.[58]

Vegan Products for Your Fridge and Pantry

We know that stocking your fridge and pantry with the most delicious products is important to making your kitchen life easy.

We prefer using organic products and unrefined ingredients whenever possible! Organic wheat and soy are at the top of our list — potatoes too. That's why we strongly recommend "organic" for those ingredients in our recipes. But we know that organic products are not always available to everyone, so do the best you can. It's so much better for your bod and for the environment!

Remember to always read labels and double check that the products you are purchasing are vegan — AND for our gluten-free friends, please double check your miso, vegan cream cheese, vegan cheeses and Worcestershire sauce, to name a few, because these products can sneak in the wheat and barley on occasion.

For your fruits and veggies — please shop at your local farmer's market or green market! You will get locally grown produce that tastes amazing at a great price, while supporting your local economy. You will also get your daily dose of vitey D from being in the sunshine, and you may make a few new friends when you're walking around.

One more quick tip — look for products that are non-hydrogenated and free of sneaky animal ingredients, like casein, monoglycerides and diglycerides, whey, gelatin, rennet, and albumen.

Here are some product recommendations that we heart!

For Your Refrigerator

Lightlife: organic soy tempeh
www.lightlife.com/index.jsp

White Wave: "chicken-style" seitan
www.tofutown.net

Miso Master: organic mellow white miso (soybean paste …
it's the light miso paste we use in our recipes)
www.great-eastern-sun.com

Nasoya: Nayonaise (non-dairy vegan mayonnaise),
and organic tofu! — www.nasoya.com

Wildwood: soymilk creamer (made from 100% U.S.-grown
organic soybeans), and baked tofu
www.pulmuonewildwood.com

Follow Your Heart makes some amazing products
we use ALL the time! — www.followyourheart.com
— Vegenaise (reduced fat non-dairy vegan mayonnaise)
— Cream Cheese and Sour Cream Alternatives line (non-hydrogenated and vegan)
— Vegan Gourmet line of cheeses

More great, melty vegan cheeses:
Daiya — www.daiyafoods.com
Teese: (P.S., they also make amazing vegan marshmallows!!!)
www.chicagosoydairy.com/products

Earth Balance: Buttery Spread (it's the "non-dairy butter" we use in our recipes ... and it's non-hydrogenated) www.earthbalancenatural.com

Aussie Bakery: puff pastry (non-hydrogenated) www.aussiebakery.com

For Your Pantry

Bob's Red Mill: our favorite for unbleached whole wheat pastry flour, arrowroot powder, and gluten-free all-purpose baking flour—www.bobsredmill.com

Arrowhead Mills: organic spelt flour, organic unbleached all-purpose flour, organic cornmeal, and vital wheat gluten (for making your own seitan!) www.arrowheadmills.com

Rudi's: spelt bread and tortillas—www.rudisbakery.com

Organic unsweetened almond or soymilk (several brands)

Spectrum Organics: refined coconut oil or safflower oil (high-heat neutral tasting oils) and spray oils for baking—www.spectrumorganics.com

Bragg: nutritional yeast and unfiltered apple cider vinegar www.bragg.com

Celtic Sea Salt—www.celticseasalt.com

Eden Brand: canned beans (these beans are canned with kombu—making them more digestible, and they have a BPA-free lining!)—www.edenfoods.com

Imagine: low-sodium vegetable broth www.imaginefoods.com

Kimberley organic wine vinegars (we love their Cabernet Sauvignon and Champagne vinegars!) www.nextgenfoods.com

Ohsawa: nigari (for making your own tofu!) www.goldminenaturalfoods.com

Ener-g: egg replacer—www.ener-g.com/egg-replacer.html

Alter Eco: unrefined ground cane sugar www.altereco-usa.com/main.php

Wholesome Sweeteners: agave nectar www.wholesomesweeteners.com

Lundberg: organic brown rice syrup—www.lundberg.com

Enjoy Life: mini chocolate chips (half the cals and fat of other choc chips!)—www.enjoylifefoods.com

Setton Farms: nuts (pistachios, cashews and more) www.settonfarms.com

The Wizard's: vegan Worcestershire sauce www.edwardandsons.com/thewizards_info.itml

San-J: tamari (gluten-free soy sauce)—www.san-j.com

Frontier Organic Spices: our fave varieties of cinnamon are Ceylon or Saigon ground cinnamon www.frontiercoop.com

Dragunara: for organic seasoning blends that add SO much flavor!—www.dragunara.com

Ginger People: pickled ginger, grated ginger www.gingerpeople.com

Make sure you are boozing vegan-style with this website: www.barnivore.com

If you live in an area where you don't have access to all of these goodies, you can stock up online!
www.veganessentials.com
www.foodfightgrocery.com
www.veganstore.com

Notes & References

We want you to have great information at your fingertips! The footnote numbers in our Sporkie Scoops refer you to food and health information found in the resource books below, as well as to other sources online.

BOOKS ON HEALTH AND DIET

Campbell, T. Colin, and Thomas M. Campbell II. *The China Study: The Most Comprehensive Study of Nutrition Ever Conducted and the Startling Implications for Diet, Weight Loss and Long-term Health.* Dallas: BenBella Books, 2006.

Collins, Elise Marie. *An A-Z Guide to Healing Foods: A Shopper's Companion.* San Francisco: Red Wheel/ Weiser, LLC, 2009.

Herbst, Sharon Tyler. *The New Food Lover's Companion: Comprehensive Definitions of Nearly 6,000 Food, Drink, and Culinary Terms.* 3rd ed. Hauppauge, NY: Barron's Educational Series, 2001.

Mateljan, George. *The World's Healthiest Foods: Essential Guide for the Healthiest Way of Eating.* Seattle: George Mateljan Foundation, 2007.

Murray, Michael T., Joseph E. Pizzorno, and Lara Pizzorno. *The Encyclopedia of Healing Foods.* New York: Atria Books, 2005.

Wood, Rebecca Theurer. *The New Whole Foods Encyclopedia: A Comprehensive Resource for Healthy Eating.* 2nd ed. New York: Penguin Books, 1999.

Wood, Rebecca Theurer. *The New Whole Foods Encyclopedia: A Comprehensive Resource for Healthy Eating.* 3rd ed. New York: Penguin Books, 2010.

NOTES

APPETIZERS

1. *The Encyclopedia of Healing Foods*, page 275.
2. www.peoplespharmacy.com/2009/09/21/celery-seed-conquers-gout-pain
3. *The Encyclopedia of Healing Foods*, page 394.
4. *The Encyclopedia of Healing Foods*, page 326.
5. www.coconut-oil-central.com/coconut-oil-osteoporosis.html
6. *The Encyclopedia of Healing Foods*, page 483.
7. www.rxlist.com/lactobacillus/supplements.htm
8. factoidz.com/the-health-benefits-of-cayenne-and-chili-peppers

SOUPS & SALADS

9. *The Science of Good Food*, page 34.
10. greekfood.about.com/od/herbsspices/p/spearmint.htm
11. www.osteopenia3.com/Food-for-bone-density.html
12. *An A-Z Guide to Healing Foods*, page 33.
13. *An A-Z Guide to Healing Foods*, page 121.
14. *The World's Healthiest Foods*, page 138.
15. *The Encyclopedia of Healing Foods*, page 436.
16. *The World's Healthiest Foods*, page 706.
17. *Healing with Whole Foods*, page 537.

SIDES

18. www.uni-graz.at/~katzer/engl/Cymb_cit.html

19. *The Encyclopedia of Healing Foods*, page 289.

20. *The Encyclopedia of Healing Foods*, page 225.

21. www.drrussellshealthandweightlossblog.com/228/hydrogenated-oil-and-transfatty-acid

22. *The World's Healthiest Foods*, page 182.

23. www.whfoods.com/genpage.php?tname=foodspice&dbid=128

24. http://www.whfoods.com/genpage.php?tname=foodspice&dbid=22

25. *The Encyclopedia of Healing Foods*, page 447.

26. *The China Study*, pages 60-61

27. *The Encyclopedia of Healing Foods*, page 173.

28. *The New Whole Foods Encyclopedia*, page 300.

29. *The New Whole Foods Encyclopedia*, page 214.

MAIN DISHES

30. *The China Study*, pages 212-213.

31. www.vegetarian-nutrition.info/updates/mighty-mushrooms.php

32. www.livestrong.com/article/111231-almond-milk-nutritional-information

33. *The Encyclopedia of Healing Foods*, page 414.

34. *The New Whole Foods Encyclopedia*, page 58.

35. *The New Whole Foods Encyclopedia*, page 297.

36. *The New Whole Foods Encyclopedia*, 2nd ed., page 33.

37. www.whfoods.com/genpage.php?tname=nutrient&dbid=116

38. *The Encyclopedia of Healing Foods*, page 501.

39. *The World's Healthiest Foods*, page 168.

40. *The World's Healthiest Foods*, page 709.

DESSERTS

41. *The New Whole Foods Encyclopedia*, page 13.

42. *The New Whole Foods Encyclopedia*, page 265.

43. *The Tao of Nutrition*, page 104.

44. *The Encyclopedia of Healing Foods*, page 667.

45. www.whfoods.com/genpage.php?tname=foodspice&dbid=101

46. *Healing with Whole Foods*, page 621.

47. *The Science of Good Food*, page 243.

48. www.blueberrysupplements.co.uk/blueberries-health-research/blueberries-urinary-tract-infections.php

49. *The New Whole Foods Encyclopedia*, page 275.

50. *The New Whole Foods Encyclopedia*, page 213.

BRUNCH

51. *The New Whole Foods Encyclopedia*, page 85.

52. www.ehow.com/how_4454257_benefit-from-nutritional-yeast.html

53. *The Tao of Nutrition*, page 28.

54. *The World's Healthiest Foods*, page 285.

55. *The Science of Good Food*, page 509.

56. factoidz.com/uses-and-health-benefits-of-nutmeg

57. *The New Food Lover's Companion*, page 551.

58. www.whfoods.com/genpage.php?tname=foodspice&dbid=72

Index

Note: (gf) indicates a gluten-free recipe

Index

(continued from previous page)

Acknowledgments

AN EXTRA SPECIAL THANK YOU TO OUR AMAZING TEAM—Patrick Gookin for his superb photography skills and Kevin Tseng for his mind-blowing art direction, attention to detail, and overall life saving! A huge thank you to the incredible and talented sisters Emily and Zooey Deschanel! And to Paul Kelly and Cathy Dees at St. Lynn's Press for their dedication to putting out meaningful, ethical and loving books!

We would like to thank our wonderful family and friends and all of our inspiring students!

A tremendous thank you to Mom, Dad, Jeremy, Grandma, Grandpa and Arlo, Wilma Engel and John Engel, Robin, Darin and Lola Mark, Wendy Wegner, Jiro Schneider, Kristin Knauff, Joshua Spencer, Casey Suchan and Denis Hennelly, Ann Hennelly, Rory Freedman, Suzanne and Al Yankovic, Tal Ronnen, Gene Baur, Sara Kramer, Nathan Hoy and EAPS, Ion, Valerie and Troy Krieger, Aunt Peanut Krieger, Aunt Jewel Brager, Mia and Harris Lee Cohen, Jessica Gelt, Lauren Virdone, Sweet Georgia Brown, Niko Hronopoulos, Heather Taylor, Hallee Gould, Mitchell Davis, Heather Monahan, Ronn Wallace and Anke Mackenthun at Spongeworks, Will Watson, Keith Manship, Professor Glenn Fieldman, Mouth Public Relations, Alyssa Smith, Farial Awan, Jagdish Vaswani, Merlin Camozzi, Kevin Hite, Zach Harris, Kevin Feyen, Sharon Galeon, Edith B. de Guzman, Stacy Grubb, Galen Goodpaster, Lauren Kaufman, Tony Yanow, Quarrygirl, Polly Walter, Heidi Spurgin at Pure Design, Holly Rosborough, Karen Masnica, Shoshana Goldhaber and the Brooklyn Goldbergs, Ryan Merchant, our lovely friends at *VegNews Magazine,* Christy Simons and Whole Foods, everyone at Nasoya, the Natural Gourmet Institute for Health and Culinary Arts, Frontier Spices, Urban Decay and Cri de Coeur.

About the Authors

Jenny Engel and Heather Goldberg are the sisters behind Spork Foods, the most popular vegan cooking school in California. Their membership-based website, sporkonline.com, gives people all over the world the opportunity to take their innovative and fun cooking classes. The Spork sisters are quickly becoming the go-to experts on the future of modern vegan cuisine. Jenny and Heather are regular contributors to *VegNews Magazine* and have received numerous accolades including a prestigious "Veggie Award." These entrepreneurial sisters have been featured in the *Los Angeles Times* and other leading print publications, and have appeared on television as cooking instructors to the stars. They reside in Los Angeles, and take a sister trip every year for inspiration.

www.sporkfoods.com   www.sporkonline.com